Where Have All the Mothers Gone?

WHERE
HAVE ALL THE MOTHERS
GONE?

DR. JEAN CHAMBERLAIN FROESE, M.D.

Stories of courage and hope during
childbirth among the world's poorest women.

Epic Press

Belleville, Ontario, Canada

Where Have All the Mothers Gone?

The illustrations that begin the chapters are the work of Heidi Scarfone (scarfone@quickclic.net), a childbirth educator and doula (www.havingyourbaby.com).

Thomas Froese and Dr. Jean Chamberlain Froese took all photos, with the exception of Dr. Chamberlain Froese delivering a child in Kiboga, Uganda, which was taken by Laura Mawson.

Editorial services were provided by Denyse O'Leary (oleary@sympatico.ca), a Toronto-based editor and writer (www.denyseoleary.com).

National Library of Canada Cataloguing in Publication
Froese, Jean Chamberlain, 1965-
   Where have all the mothers gone? / Jean Chamberlain Froese.
Includes bibliographical references.
ISBN 1-55306-762-2 / 978-1-55306-762-7

   1. Maternal health services--Africa. 2. Mothers--Africa--Mortality. I. Title.
RG966.A1F76 2004   362.1'982'0096   C2003-906877-3

Epic Press is an imprint of *Essence Publishing*.
For more information, contact:
20 Hanna Court, Belleville, Ontario, Canada K8P 5J2.
Phone: 1-800-238-6376 • Fax: (613) 962-3055.
E-mail: info@essence-publishing.com
Internet: www.essence-publishing.com

For my mother…

Table of Contents

Every day, 1,600 women in the developing world die from preventable complications of pregnancy and childbirth. Walk
through an overview of this grim, yet often unreported, global
tragedy, and prepare for the author's moving, first-hand stories.

God's hands are our hands, as He seeks to care for His beloved
daughters in childbirth.

In poverty-stricken rural East Africa, nature often runs its
course. A woman is not brought to a hospital until she and her
baby are already in mortal danger. Such delays are common
when social and cultural myths of health care prevail. Dr. Jean
learns the hard way.

Foreword

Speaking as one who has been involved in Africa for more than 40 years, has lived there for 17 years, and has visited half of its nations, I am convinced that this book is a "Must Read" for anyone who wants to know the facts about how mothers fare there.

Dr. Chamberlain Froese's experience, both on the ground and in the developing world, as well as with significant professional organizations, makes her particularly well qualified to talk about mothers who slip through the cracks. She is also well qualified to challenge the status quo and lead in bringing about change.

When she talks about the 585,000 unnecessary deaths that take place yearly, she is sounding an alarm we must all heed, with heart as well as mind.

When you read this book, and hear the stories of mothers who have only just survived—and some who have not—you will understand why she has thrown her life and passion into what God has called her to do.

This book will stir you deeply!

Cal R. Bombay
Vice President
Crossroads Christian Communications Inc.
Burlington, Ontario
Canada

Special Thanks from Jean

I would like to thank all of the women and men who have told me the stories of their experiences in caring for mothers in developing countries. To mention a few: Dr. Florence Mirembe (Uganda), Dr. Anthony Mugasa (Uganda), and Dorraine Ross (Zambia / Canada). A special thanks to Dr. Paul and Pedrinah Thistle, of Howard Hospital, Zimbabwe, for their efforts and insights. I so much appreciate the talent and efforts of Heidi Scarfone, my illustrator, and Denyse O'Leary who tirelessly edited this book. Of course, this book would not have been possible were it not for my journalist husband and best friend Thomas Froese, who pushed forward and made it happen.

Mothers Are Dying...

From the time you had your morning coffee today until the same time tomorrow, 1,470 women will have died from complications of pregnancy and childbirth. Most of these women (86%) lived in sub-Saharan Africa and Asia. Annually, the global community looses 525,000 mothers from primarily preventable pregnancy complications.[1] A mother's (and her child's) chance of dying from pregnancy complications depends primarily on her geography. Put another way, one out of every 22 women in sub-Saharan Africa will die from a pregnancy-related complication. In the industrialized world, 1 in 8,000 women will die.[2]

Consider twenty-two of your female acquaintances. If they lived under the conditions of Africa, one of your friends would be destined to die from maternity complications. By contrast, most North Americans and Europeans will simply never know a woman who dies in such a manner.

Incredibly, in the 20th century, this stubborn scourge killed more than tuberculosis, suicide, traffic accidents or AIDS. More women died from childbirth complications than the number of men killed in either of the world wars.

Approximately four million neomnatal deaths and still-births are caused by inadequate maternal care during pregnancy and delivery.[3] This means that annually, 4.5 million deaths are attributed to poor materal care (525,000 mothers and 4 million neonatal deaths/stillborns). These dead women also leave many children without mothers. And many of the women who do survive childbirth develop a fistula, a torn birth canal that leaves them incontinent of stool or urine: women who will be thrown out of their families and villages, like lepers.

Women's lifetime risks of dying from pregnancy-related complications (WHO, UNICEF, UNFPA estimates 2000) [4]

Region	Risk of Dying
Sub-Saharan Africa	1 in 22
North Africa and Middle East	1 in 140
Latin America and Caribbean	1 in 280
East Asia and Pacific	1 in 350
Developing countries	1 in 76
Industrialized countries	1 in 8,000

CAUSES of Maternal Mortality [5] (% of total maternal deaths)

Severe bleeding	25%
Infection	15%
Unsafe abortion	13%
High blood pressure	12%

Obstructed labour	8%
Other direct causes	8%
Other indirect causes	20%

The largest cause of maternal mortality is severe bleeding. One in four deaths results from haemorrhaging that can often be prevented by medication costing less than a coffee. Other causes include infection (15%) and high blood pressure in pregnancy (12%). Most of these causes are preventable.

At the heart of the issue is that about half of all women in developing countries don't have a skilled birth attendant at their delivery. They may have an untrained traditional birth attendant, or their mother-in-law. Or they may be on their own.

A global picture [6]

Region	% of Deliveries With a Skilled Attendant*
Global	63%
Africa	46%
*Eastern Africa	34%
Asia	61%
Latin America	88%
Europe	99%
North America	99%

The death of a mother severely reduces the chance of her child's survival. The death of one mother and her infant often leaves a family of orphans. When a mother dies, her surviving children are 3 to 10 times more likely to die within two years than children who live with both parents.[7]

...but many can be saved!

The hindrances to maternal care are many, yet none are impossible to overcome. They include distance from health services, finances (cost of treatment, transportation), lack of drugs and supplies, excessive demands on women's time, and women's lack of decision-making power within their families. In certain situations, the treatment provided by the health care team is substandard, and so it is shunned by pregnant mothers.

Yet, all pregnant mothers should have access to emergency obstetrical care. This care includes trained midwives who will provide services at village posts. It is preferable to have local women trained as midwives to ensure their commitment to the region. These midwives need a functional referral system when they must transfer a patient in trouble. This means that a hospital with competent physicians and staff are ready to receive and treat complicated patients.

In addition, the referral system requires both a communication component (e.g., two-way radio) and emergency transportation (e.g., motorized ambulance, cycles or a roster of local vehicles to be designated for this purpose). Outpost clinics and hospitals must be stocked with a reliable source of drugs and equipment. Coca-Cola successfully reaches these remote areas!

More controversial yet plausible strategies include the training of outpost nurses to perform Caesarean sections and the use of maternity houses, which are close to health facilities.

One strategy will not meet all the needs within a community. A wholistic plan must be tailored to the individual district. The community must be mobilized and take a significant stand on the importance of safe motherhood. It needs to be seen as a social norm and not a random happening.

Women, themselves, must be better educated and gain increasing power over their own health choices. The local and national governments need to take active steps in elevating the status of women within their district and country. The media is an important tool to educate the public and lobby for mothers' health and rights.

This book was written to mobilize help for our neighbours in what is, after all, a shrinking world. As the stories of mothers around the world are told, whether tragic deaths or narrow escapes, perhaps the telling can lead to broader change.

Consider the terribly unequal distribution of wealth on this planet. Almost 90 per cent of Earth's 6.1 billion human beings live in the developing world, yet in 2004, not a single member government[8] of the G-8 has given foreign aid up to the recognized target of 0.7 per cent of their Gross Domestic Product (GDP)[9]. The world's richest 20% receive 74% of the global income while the poorest 20% receive a meagre 2% of the global pot.[10]

As you read the stories of these brave mothers in developing countries, try and imagine how their stories would have been different if there was a greater resolve and better infrastructure to protect the lives of these women and their children.

References

[1] Maternal Mortality in 2005. Estimates developed by WHO, UNICEF, UNFPA and the World Bank. WHO, Geneva, pg. 1. Available at www.unfpa.org/publications

[2] *Ibid.*, pg. 35

[3] World Health Organization: *Mother-Baby Package: Implementing Safe Motherhood in Countries.*

[4] Maternal Mortality in 2005. Estimates developed by WHO, UNICEF, UNFPA and the World Bank. WHO, Geneva, pg. 1. Available at www.unfpa.org/publications

[5] AbouZahr C. Global burden of maternal death and disability. In: Rodeck C, ed. *Reducing maternal death and disability in pregnancy.* Oxford, Oxford University Press, 2003: 1-11.

6 WHO, department of Reproductive Health and Research. Proportions of births attended to be a skilled attendant—2007 updates. Fact Sheet. WHO, Geneva. Available on-line at http://www.who.int/reproductive-health/global_monitoring/

7 World Health Organization: Safe Motherhood as a Vital Social and Economic Investment. Geneva, 1998.

8 Human Development Report 2006 UNDP pg. 343. Available at http://hdr.undp.org/

9 Copson, Raymond. CRS Report for Congress: Africa, the G8 and the Blair Initiative. Congressional Research Service. the Library of Congress. June 2005, pg. 3.

10 Human Development Report 2006 UNDP. Available at http://undp.org/

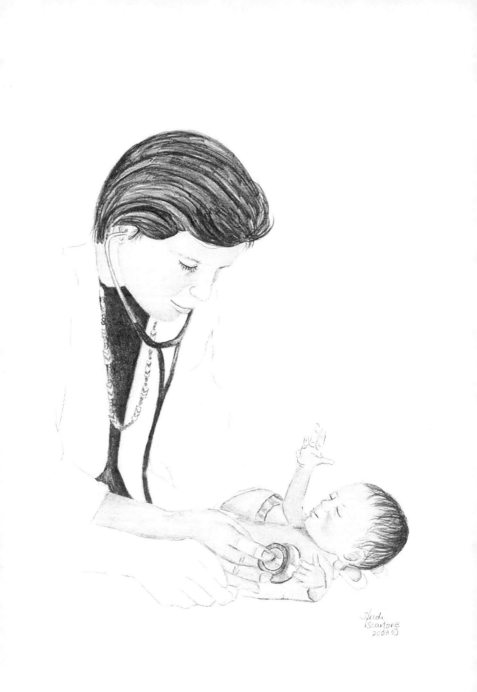

CHAPTER ONE

Alone... Where Is the Presence of God?

Alone in a dark corridor, I could not escape this hurting girl, even if I wanted to. Our ears were teased by the hum of African drums, beating outside the hospital compound. As the clock struck 1 a.m., she moaned in pain and misery.

Both the father of her baby and her family had deserted her. At the age of 16, she was left alone to give birth. It would not be a natural birth. Her body had not had time to develop fully. She faced Caesarean section—and motherhood—alone.

I cried out to God, "Where are you at this moment? Can't you hear her? I do not understand her frantic words, her chants, her moaning."

I rubbed her back and spoke softly to her. There was nothing more I could do. I am a doctor, but not a miracle worker. I need tools and the expertise of other professionals to do my work.

The night watchman was frantically searching for the anaesthesia assistant, who could give this poor girl a temporary respite from her lonely hell.

She lurched forward again—another painful contraction was starting. I continued to stroke her back. I clutched her hand.

Beads of sweat formed on her forehead. Drops of perspiration flowed down my own back. My surgical uniform was soaked with her tears.

I looked nervously down the hall. Where were my co-workers?

I continued my conversation with God. "Dear God, where are you? Where is your comfort for this young child of yours? Please stop her pain, and comfort her troubled soul."

I was desperate, yet the heavens were silent.

Then He whispered, "My child, your hands are my hands. Your voice is my voice. Your presence is my presence. My hands have been stroking her painful back, and my voice has been calming her soul."

Finally, help arrived. The anaesthetic equipment started its predictable hum. A few moments later, the young girl slept.

Her ordeal was over for now. But I had learned an important lesson: My God was present, not in a white cloud or mighty voice, but in tenderness and compassion offered to this helpless girl.

She delivered a beautiful little girl with curly black hair, another human being made in the image of God. One to whom the presence of God can be made known by the hands He gave me.

It was no surprise that the young mother did not remember me when I visited her on the maternity ward a few days later. The trauma, the agony, and the terror seemed distant now. She didn't recall those to whom she had entrusted her life during a helpless—and hopeless—moment.

I too quickly forget the provision and presence of God in my life, in times of distress and loneliness.

One form of heroism, the most common, and yet the least remembered of all—namely, the heroism of the average mother!

—CHARLES KINGSLEY

Death Seizes an Opportunity

I n the delivery room, she seemed like a typical "first time" mother. She looked 17 but her chart said that she was 24. The people who had brought her told me that she had gone into labour 12 hours before, and that they had brought her from the remote village to the hospital because her labour was slowing down. I believed them.

I was wrong. I should not have been so naïve. As I learned later, the truth is that most women who are transferred to the hospital in this way have seen at least two sunsets since their labour began. The "twelve hours" was just a figure that people gave, in order to avoid arousing the anger of the hospital midwives. ("Why didn't you bring her earlier? You must have realized that something was wrong!")

The young woman herself did not dare tell me. After all, if she lived, she would have to go home again.

I examined her. At the time, there were no obvious warning signs. I assured both the patient and the midwife that I would return in two hours to assess her progress. If her labour was continuing in a normal way, we could hope for a normal delivery. Otherwise, we would have to do a Caesarean section.

We listened to the baby's heart. It clicked at 150 beats per minute, perfectly normal. There was no cause for concern.

The young African doctors and I started the maternity rounds, seeing the patients on the ward. Suddenly, a frantic midwife burst through the swinging doors. The young patient whom we had just seen had gone into convulsions.

We all stopped in mid-sentence and dashed around the corner to the labour suite. We braced ourselves for what we would find. Would the patient be foaming at the mouth? Shaking uncontrollably? Fallen off of the bed?

By the time we got there, it appeared that the worst was over. Her eyes stared blankly at the ceiling. Her body was still. This is called a "post-ictal" state, and it is common after a grand mal seizure. Her mother stood at the head of the bed, rigid with terror. At that point it was hard to be sure who needed more help, the mother-to-be or the grandmother-to-be.

But one thing was clear. Natural childbirth was not an option. The longer delivery was postponed, the more likely this young woman would have another seizure.

The midwife quickly administered Valium by intravenous, to prevent further seizures as we moved the patient to the operating theatre.

Unfortunately, the most effective anti-seizure drug for pregnant patients was not available in this rural African hospital. We would just have to make do with what was in stock.

It is not easy to mobilize an operating room staff within a few minutes. Workers scrambled to assemble the necessary equipment and the security guard went to find the anaesthesia assistant, to put the patient under.

A nurse scribbled down a consent for surgery, not from the

patient—she was not able to make an informed decision—but from her mother. The shaken grandmother could not read or write English, but the nurse explained the necessary treatment, and a thumbprint would suffice. She only wanted what was best for her daughter.

As we all scrambled, the minutes ticked away. The young mother stopped seizing. She was almost conscious when the anaesthetic began to work. I wasn't familiar with the smell of ether myself; it is no longer routinely used in Western hospitals. I heard the young anaesthesia assistant shout loud and clear: "Doctors, you may start."

A tall, young African physician stood across the surgical table from me. We adjusted the table for his height, and I stood on tiptoes throughout the procedure. I was really there to help him learn to do this procedure.

I wondered what the outcome for the mother and baby would be. The baby must have suffered from lack of oxygen during the seizure. Would this little one make it? We would soon know. It was only a minute before the baby's head was delivered.

There was no hiding the truth now. This mother had been in labour for *several days.* The shape of the baby's head told us that much.

We passed the baby to the midwife as quickly as possible. I did not even get a chance to see if it was a boy or girl. We had to focus on stopping the mother's bleeding.

I could hear the midwife and anaesthesia assistant working with the baby over in the infant resuscitation corner. But we heard no cries. Not a good sign. I called over my shoulder, asking, was there anything I could do?

Not really. The staff were doing the right things, but nothing was happening. The minutes clicked on. No response. No life. Well, at least we had tried everything we could.

The midwife came over and told us that the baby had been

a boy. He appeared to have a genetic disorder which included a cleft palate and an abnormal upper lip.

It would all be hard news to break to the mother when she woke up. After all that suffering, no baby to cuddle.

We completed the surgery, and I snapped my gloves into the waste bin. Surgeons have feelings, and sometimes the feeling is sadness. No new little voice would be heard in this young woman's hut. Not only would she suffer grief, but also the ridicule that is often heaped on African women who experience an unsuccessful pregnancy. The social pressures from her neighbours and friends would be intense. She had "failed" as a first time mother. I bitterly remembered the old saying, "A woman will always sacrifice herself if you give her the opportunity. It is her favourite form of self-indulgence."

However, I also recognized that if this mother had stayed in her village much longer, she would have died too. At least she was not another addition to the pitiful maternal mortality statistics of this district. At least she now had another chance at life, both for herself and her future children. In that way, we had succeeded.

But next time, she needed to come to us earlier, and not fear modern medicine, but rather embrace it as the best hope for her future. How can we get the message across?

In a society where the rights and potentials of women
are constrained, no man can be truly free.
He may have power, but he will not have freedom.

—MARY ROBINSON, FORMER PRESIDENT OF IRELAND

CHAPTER THREE

Margaret—the Traditional Midwife

Her eyes met mine. And I liked her instantly.

Her name was Margaret. No doubt this fact endeared her to me immediately, because that is my mother's name too. But there the similarities between my mother's life and hers ended.

The young Ugandan woman had a warm, spunky personality and an obvious enthusiasm for her work. In some ways, she reminded me of myself. Her features resembled mine, high cheekbones on a thin face. She wore her hair short, as I did.

There were differences. I wore a plain blue cotton dress; she wore a colourful Ugandan print made of cool polyester. My skin was white; hers was brown. I spoke English; she spoke Lugandan.

Despite the barriers in communication, we had a lively discussion about Margaret's work as a traditional birth attendant (TBA) or midwife in the region of Mmwero, Uganda.

She talked at some length about the challenges she faced as a TBA. My main concern was that her fellow TBA (who was attempting to translate) would miss some of Margaret's key insights as she described maternity out in the villages.

Occasionally, as Margaret paused for a breath, the translator shifted her eyes to mine while relaying the message in English. I kept watching Margaret's eyes.

My concentrated gaze may have conveyed the mistaken impression that I had understood every word. No matter that I couldn't. I could piece together the facts and figures through the well-intentioned effort of our translator and friend.

Margaret told me about the disrespect that a TBA suffered from the local women and, more importantly, the village men. Pregnant mothers preferred to go to a TBA such as herself rather than to a professionally trained midwife or a hospital, yet they would not pay for birth attendant services. Her clients' husbands would give her vegetables or fruit or a handful of cash (equivalent to $2 to $3 US) that nowhere near repaid the many hours she had spent with the woman at her delivery.

Worse, she explained angrily, the TBA had to pay for her own surgical gloves and equipment, costs not covered by the pittance the husband tossed her. She begged me to provide her with a steady supply of gloves.

The conversation took a more positive turn. Margaret proudly displayed the list of deliveries she had carried out over the past five years.

But the page that documented her successful deliveries was less than half full. Five deliveries in the first year, four the next and the numbers continued to go down. She had successfully delivered only one baby the year before. Why the decline?

Would she be able to keep up her skills properly, with such a small patient population? Or was I missing something? Something I didn't know or understand. Possibly she was blind to the reasons herself. Had she lost the confidence of her patients?

She obviously cared for mothers as I did. But she could not read or write. At the seminar at which I met her, a trained midwife had assisted her in filling out the questionnaire I had helped to design.

So here we were, me with twelve years of university training and Margaret, who was illiterate, miles apart in one sense, yet side-by-side in another: linked with a love for our fellow women and anxious to find ways to ensure their safe delivery.

Maternity care is like walking across Niagara Falls on a chain rope. Each link in the chain is one component.

The first link is village level care. That link is my TBA friend Margaret, providing limited, yet loving, care. If she delays sending a patient in distress to the hospital, it could mean death or severe consequences.

The second link is transportation, the vital bond between the village and emergency obstetrical services at a hospital. If no bus, car, or even bicycle is available, Margaret would be left with a certain maternal death.

The final link is hospital care. Is it adequate, safe, and available both day and night? A maternity unit that is functional for only nine hours a day is a recipe for disaster. Can I train young physicians to carry out safe maternity care, to treat carefully and operate skillfully? Can they be motivated to provide assistance day and night?

Margaret and I must link arms to ensure safe delivery for Ugandan mothers. We must trust one another. I must be able to believe the report that she gives of a mother's progression in labour, and she must rely on my judgment, believing that I will only intervene when necessary.

A trusting relationship between maternity caregivers takes time to build. Friendships are not grown in a day, but this morning was an opportunity to gaze into the eyes of another who shared the dream and love for African mothers. We are miles apart in education, wealth, and cultural experiences, yet we are equal links in a chain to help young women cross safely to motherhood.

> *Kindness is the golden chain*
> *by which society is bound together.*
>
> —JOHANN VON GOETHE

CHAPTER FOUR

Motorcycle Annie—the Rural Midwife with Power Assist

They called her Annette; they could have called her the Life Saver. This African woman was the local midwife, health consultant, social worker—and joy giver—all in one, in her community in Zambia's copper belt.

In that community, more than 50 children were orphans as a result of AIDS and pregnancy complications. They had no home, and little opportunity to learn the culture and values they needed to grow up peacefully among their African neighbours.

Annette came to the rescue by helping to find them families. Meanwhile, her close friend Betty helped educate them. These women could not afford to pay school fees, but they could teach the little ones to read and write using the chalkboard and benches at the local church during the week, when it wasn't in use. Annette was always looking for ways to improve their quality of life.

She spent the rest of her time operating the local health care facility in her isolated community, a nine-hour drive north of

Lusaka, Zambia's capital. Her clinic was originally set up only as a maternity unit, but because there was no other health professional for 30 km, pretty well anyone with a need showed up on the clinic's doorstep. It was hard to turn away a man with a slashed hand or broken foot. After all, it wasn't his fault that he wasn't pregnant!

The two aides on duty at the clinic were always busy: they took blood pressures, measured the growth of unborn babies, and prepared women for their deliveries. Most local women were anemic, so they had low red blood cell counts. A bout of malaria might kill them.

Annette ran a tight ship. About 50 women delivered their children in the cramped maternity unit every month. She had some basic equipment: two delivery beds, a fetal stethoscope, and instruments such as clamps and scissors. Annette was careful to sterilize all her equipment between patients. Contagious diseases, especially AIDS, were all too common. The orderliness and cleanliness of her clinic showed the pride she took in her work.

In between pregnant patients, she might squeeze in others: a case of gastritis or a sore ankle, for example. People would walk for miles to consult her. The reputation of a competent health care worker is highly valued in this part of the world. Besides, Annette had a telling smile and gentle attitude toward even the most pathetic of patients.

The night began to settle in. Soon she would be home, preparing dinner. Annette was married to a schoolteacher, and after 18 years of marriage, she still loved him and enjoyed preparing dinner. They had five children. Her two daughters helped with dinner, especially when she was late at the clinic. Tonight, they would have cabbage, rice and a small luxury, beef, because it was her wedding anniversary. They would prepare the food over the fire pit at the back of their small house.

Annette was just about ready to turn out the light and leave the clinic when she heard footsteps and voices outside the door. It was the husband of one of her prenatal patients and another man. Both were out of breath. They were carrying Jane, the pregnant wife, in a hammock.

Tonight's plans for a quiet dinner at home would have to be rearranged.

Annette knew that, for these men to travel so far, the problem must be serious. Of Jane's six previous pregnancies, two children did not survive long. Jane didn't really know why they died; few women in those parts did. Villagers did not even name a newborn until it was at least a week old.

"Welcome, my friends," Annette said warmly to the two struggling men.

"My wife has had no baby, and it has been many days. We decided to bring her here as she is starting to talk nonsense and I do not know what to do with her," said her husband Peter.

"I am glad that you have come. You're a wise father. You must be tired. Please place her on the bed back here; then come and sit, and have a soda."

"For that, I need no encouragement," he replied, as they placed Jane on an iron bed in a delivery room.

Annette always kept a supply of sodas in the clinic for moments such as this. African men always seemed willing to accept a Coca-Cola while they waited. She examined her patient. Jane was dehydrated, weak, and mostly incoherent, her face dripping with sweat.

Annette reached for the fetal stethoscope. The baby was dead. Annette was disappointed, but not surprised. Jane would be dead soon too, if treatment was not started immediately.

Jane began to thrash in pain from the strong but useless contractions. Annette noticed something else, wet leaves on the bed. Jane had used traditional medicines to initiate her labour, a technique that had probably made things worse.

The sun had set. Annette knew that Jane would never see it rise again if she did not somehow get to the mission hospital 30 kilometres away. It was not just any 30 kilometres. Between Jane and Mukinge Hospital were pothole-ridden dirt roads that challenged even the best of Land Rovers.

Annette did not have a Land Rover. She had a Suzuki motorbike that she had recently bought with four years of savings. It wasn't sophisticated, but it might do.

"Dear sir, your wife must go to the hospital quickly. We cannot delay," Annette said to the man on the wooden bench.

Her husband winced.

"I have no way to take her there," he whispered quietly, embarrassed. It was shameful not to provide for one's family. Still, to transport his wife to the hospital so many miles away, especially in the dead of the night...

"Don't worry. I will take her on my motorbike. I am sorry that we cannot take you also. I can usually fit three, but your wife is pregnant and big," Annette explained.

Then the long night ride began. Annette strapped Jane upright to the bike, and tied her to herself. It was not comfortable for a pregnant and sick woman, but it was as safe as could be hoped for. Off they roared. Annette was happy to recall that she had put some diesel into the bike's hungry tank just a few days earlier.

The dim headlight of the bike gave just enough light to see large potholes, and warn Annette if any of the bridges were washed out.

Jane moaned with discomfort as they rocked and rolled down the road. Annette prayed for God's help and protection. Wild animals could so easily bring a tragic end to her efforts. She was concerned as Jane became weaker. What if the labouring woman slipped off the bike? She clutched Jane's leg with her left hand and steered with her right.

Annette had driven this road many times, yet this trip seemed longer than usual. The bright African moon helped illuminate the roadway. A beautiful array of stars reminded her that she was not alone. Her mind wandered home. She saw her husband and children around the dinner table enjoying the feast that was meant to celebrate her wedding anniversary.

Another groan from Jane quickly jerked her back to the task at hand.

At the hospital entrance, one light bulb shone dimly, but Annette knew where to go anyway. She had trained at the hospital and had often been back. The night watchman helped her with Jane, who was now limp. They each swung an arm over one of their shoulders and dragged her to a bed in the maternity unit.

Jane received immediate surgery to remove the dead baby. Fortunately, she lived. Her four children at home were not left alone, but their mother was restored to them after a very close call.

Annette was crowned "Motorcycle Annie," on her anniversary night.

Each woman is far from average in the daily heroics
of her life, even though she may never receive
a moment's recognition in history.

—Maya V. Patel

CHAPTER FIVE

Doctor, I've Been Pregnant for Two Years!

The young African physician was much too polite to laugh at Geraldine, a peasant woman. Some people would have. Hers was certainly a strange complaint.

He simply asked her to describe what she meant. Pregnant for two years?

Five years earlier, she had married a banana farmer in central Uganda. To her, he was a catch. Most eligible men seemed to be taken. In fact, all eight of her sisters were married, so she felt a lot of pressure to catch up with the rest.

But despite her fear of being the "old maid," she was determined to be her husband's only wife. A woman whose husband had other wives faced troubles she did not want.

So she prayed, and God had answered her prayer, in the form of a simple but loving man named Isaac. The physician moved in his seat, but allowed her to continue her drawn-out story.

Geraldine did not seem to know much about pregnancy. She did know, however, that her normal monthly bleeding would stop once she conceived. So, each month she awaited the feeling of life moving within her. But, again and again, she was disappointed by the start of a new cycle. Finally a month arrived when she had no bleeding. As the days dragged on, she was certain two months had passed.

The months continued to pass, and her abdomen began to increase. She would proudly rub her abdomen in the sight of her friends at the market. Some thought that she was expecting twins. This prospect gave her great happiness. At one time, there had been a stigma around the birth of twins in her village, but not any more. She would deliver two healthy baby boys for her patient husband. "I will be the mother of many," she proudly announced.

This sent a rumble of giggles throughout the gathering of women. It seemed that she had been pregnant a very long time. Yes, she might be having twins, but when?

Patiently, she continued to carry out her duties as wife and farmer. Despite what the other women were thinking, this pregnancy could not be a figment of her imagination!

Over 26 months came and went. The delivery date just never seemed to come. Her babies were so very still. She consulted the traditional birth attendant, who could only say that she must have very lazy babies. At last, Geraldine realized that she would have to go to a pregnancy clinic in a nearby village.

She walked the three kilometres to the midwife's clinic. She was disappointed that the midwife did not tell her the answer. Far from it, the midwife said that Geraldine's case was too complicated for her. She recommended that Geraldine go to a medical doctor.

Far from discouraging her, Isaac said he would go with her, as he was going to the city anyway. So they arrived at the large cement hospital early in the morning. The university teaching centre was huge, unfamiliar, and imposing. Geraldine began to think she was crazy to come here.

At the obstetric department, women were perched in a long line on wooden benches, waiting to see the physician. Geraldine urged Isaac to go and do the business that he had planned. She would be at least three to four hours in this line, and longer if wealthier women cheated their way to the front. She dared not complain. She simply clung to the edge of the bench and shuffled close to the woman in front of her.

After hours, Geraldine's patience was rewarded. She finally sat with the doctor. Better still, he seemed gentle and kind, not the stern and powerful man that she had expected. He listened to her story.

Now perhaps she would get an answer. Why had she been pregnant so long? When would she deliver these children?

After the doctor had examined her, he gently asked her to sit down in the chair by his desk. His face was kind, but his news was bad. She was not pregnant. Something else was causing the swelling.

"Please sir, I want so much to have children," she replied. "Please make me have a child."

"Little mama, we will do surgery and find out the reason. I will do all that I can to help you. I can assure you of this."

The doctor went on to explain that she would be made to fall asleep and that he would then look inside her. Most of his words did not register, but his plan was her only hope. She would have to trust his judgment. Isaac had returned in time to hear what the city doctor had said, and he agreed.

It was a very nervous night on the female ward for Geraldine, more than for most patients. Everything about the sterile hospital seemed strange. The nurses awakened her in the middle of the night to place a warm glass stick under her arm. Then they removed it a few minutes later, only to write something on the paper that hung on the rail at the end of her bed.

Worst of all, she was not permitted to eat. She could not

even drink her tea in the morning. She couldn't recall so strange and uncomfortable a day in her life.

Finally, the nurse prepared her for the operation. She was rolled to the operating theatre on a long, stainless steel stretcher. She could not understand why she couldn't just walk in. She was in good health, fit to climb the steepest hills in Uganda.

Geraldine recalled nothing of the surgery. She awakened to the smile of the surgeon and the recovery room nurse. Then she gazed down at her abdomen. It was flat.

She looked up at the doctor. He explained, "Your abdomen was filled with fluid and a large ball or cyst that was attached to your ovary. I took out both the ovary and the cyst, and now you will be fine."

What a strange story, she thought. But the medications clouded her thinking. She would understand more later.

Geraldine recovered quickly. Before she knew it, she was back in her village. The work was hard, but that did not matter. Surely a baby would come now. She would show the mocking crowd that she was indeed a capable woman. A baby in her arms would prove that.

After a year, she missed her monthly cycle. She was delighted. And this time, her symptoms were different. She felt her whole body change. Some days were difficult, because the morning sickness lasted all day. She dared not complain. This was for what she had waited.

But Isaac was concerned about her. He thought she should go and stay in the capital, Kampala, with his relatives. There she could see the doctor who had helped them so much before.

The doctor was surprised to see her again, not because she was pregnant but because she had spent money and made the effort to see him. He would not charge this poor peasant family for his services, but the hospital fees would somehow have to be paid.

On a Friday evening, Geraldine delivered a healthy baby boy, with no troubles and no complaint. Her dream had become a reality. She was discharged from the hospital with the love of her life gurgling in her arms. She could see the pride in her husband's step as he walked beside her down the dusty road. Geraldine knew that she would never forget the gentle physician who had helped her so much, or the hospital of which she had learned not to be afraid.

Unfortunately, things went badly for Uganda during the years when her son was a child. The terror launched by Idi Amin touched all Ugandans.

Geraldine's village was not hit as hard as some. She was careful to remain indoors at night and she did not allow the reckless soldiers who frequented the beer halls in her village to even glimpse her son. Alcohol could turn a man with a rifle over his shoulder into a savage who had no respect for the innocent. Each night she prayed that God would have mercy on her people and stop this insanity. Until then, all she could do was protect and provide, and continue to pray.

Meanwhile, the physician continued to work steadily in the maternity unit. New lives were born every day despite the upheaval in the capital. He went directly to work every day, and avoided any distractions. He hoped that his "good behaviour" would protect him from misguided militia or a discontented official. Sometimes these officials vented their anger on medical personnel.

As familiar as living in fear became, he never entirely got used to it. But the babies refused to wait for a better time to be born. He would quietly ask each new little life he delivered, "Do you know what you are heading into?" They answered him only by crying, to express their dislike of the cooler air in the outside world.

One hot day, he stopped by the local restaurant to spend a few moments with friends and enjoy a cold drink. Shots rang out. Everyone dove for the floor. His friend crashed heavily against the wooden chair. The doctor felt a twinge in his left leg—he would look after that later, if he lived.

The rampage seemed to be over almost as soon as it started. Had the gunman done what he had planned? Would he go away now? Was it safe to peer over the tables?

Slowly, stunned people crept to their knees. The doctor gazed down. His brown cotton pants were wet with blood. He had been hit, but unlike his friend he was alive to tell the story.

A bystander took him to the hospital, the very hospital where he was accustomed to give assistance to others. Equipment was scarce, as he well knew, but still, he would need to have the bullet removed. Recovery would be a ways off, and he would also be mourning the death of a friend.

The untraceable line of news is a wonder of Africa. It is active even in time of war. Within a week, the news of the physician's tragedy reached Geraldine's village. She was in tears. She wailed as only a village mother can. She would have to do something to help this man who had helped her so much.

Early the next morning, she caught the commuter bus and headed for Kampala. She spent two days wages to pay the fare and used her special savings to buy him some fruit and a tattered but colourful get-well card. She arrived at the hospital mid-afternoon, and eventually located his room in the huge maze of concrete.

Geraldine quietly tiptoed in. She was embarrassed, conscious of her lack of education and social position, compared to this man. How would he react? Would he think she was pretentious, simply arriving on his doorstep like this, after a number of years?

Her fears were quickly relieved. She saw a warm smile on the face of the man that she so much admired.

He was astounded by her generosity, and her heartfelt wishes for his recovery and health. He had cared for thousands of patients over the years, yet she was the first one to come back and care about him. He also knew the risk that she took in traveling so far during this dangerous time.

Tears of gratitude welled up in his eyes. She, who had little, had given him much. Her "get-well" card would remain in his collection of treasured gifts and mementos of his life in medicine.

Even war could not quench the authentic love of a mother for her child, and for her respectful caregiver.

> *Motherhood has its marvellous power, and in it is*
> *blended pain and joy, at once the deepest*
> *and the most cleansing influence in the world.*
>
> —THE NEW YORK TIMES, MAY 10, 1929

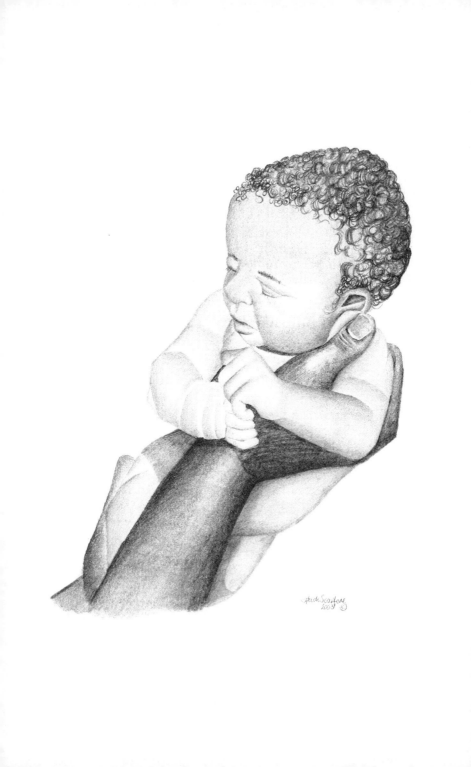

Chapter Six

A Late Delivery

Sophia was so sure that she had the world by the tail. Gathered around her were her five beautiful children. Their teeth sparkled in the moonlight as they gathered around the open fire.

"Another day is going to rest my little ones," she whispered as she got up from the fire pit. "You too must get some sleep, to be sharp to hear all that the teacher will tell you tomorrow. Make your father and me proud of your work."

The children knew what she meant. They scattered in every direction to get ready for bed. They all ended up back in the hut, ready for dreams.

Often, these days, they dreamed about modern life. Glorious fruits, delicious foods, an endless supply of fresh water, and even electricity.

In their village, that was a fantasy. But a few of their relatives had achieved it. And it was a hope for them to cling to.

On many occasions, Sophia whispered, "Work hard, and

one day you too will enjoy these things. The beautiful African sky has no limit for my children."

Sophia was proud of her little ones and she lived on a tight budget to ensure that their school fees were paid. Sometimes she earned money by cleaning the offices of the local village counsel. They didn't pay much, and sometimes it took them two months to get around to paying her. But every shilling helped.

The new morning's sun soon peaked over the African hills. The beautiful red against the shimmering orange background was a welcome sight for even the sleepiest of the children.

"Time to rise, my little George," she whispered in the ear of one late young sleeper. "Put on your school uniform and have some hot tea and a chapatti. I have made them for you. Eat with your brother, then take him to his school on your way. You must not be late."

The young boy limped to his feet and stumbled out the mud frame door. The children had to be on their way by 7:00 a.m. George had to trust his mother for the time because she was the only one who had a watch.

Sophia could imagine no greater joy than what she experienced now, watching her five children walking hand-in-hand down the path toward the schools that would prepare them for life. She paused to enjoy her moment of triumph—the desire of every African woman—success in childbearing and watching her children grow up healthy and successful.

Sophia had assumed that her family of five was complete. She was careful to get her family planning injection from the local clinic, almost all of the time.

However, just recently, she had missed one.

Well, under the circumstances, it might have happened to anyone. Her favourite sister was visiting, and the usual routines were all forgotten.

Now, she began to think that she might be pregnant. The

months passed. The rainy season came and went. It became apparent that she *was* pregnant.

At first, she did not think much about it. This year's crop was successful. The main thing was that they would have another prosperous year. This unexpected little one was welcome, even though there would be financial strain over the school fees.

Sophia wondered if the expected new baby would be as smart as George or as gentle as Kitiwie. She was certain that it was a boy. Boys were always latecomers.

Sophia continued to work into late pregnancy. As the sun shone warmly on the fertile Ugandan soil, her head covering provided some relief from the intense blaze. But she still longed for the rain, both to cool her, and to water the crop.

One day, after a few hours of work in the fields, she stopped at the market to buy some fish to prepare lunch for her husband. As usual, she also picked up sticks on the walk home from the market. The children never seemed to find enough to keep the fire burning. Before long, the fish was simmering in greasy Blue Bonnet margarine. Sophia was grateful that Humphrey was a wise and understanding man. She knew women who had done worse.

Then, suddenly, an all-too-familiar feeling interrupted their meal. Sophia knew that she would soon be in labour. She was used to the usual discomforts and pains of pregnancy, but for some reason this one felt different. The baby seemed to be lying differently and pressed on parts of her anatomy in ways she had never experienced before.

Sophia intended to deliver this baby at the local maternity clinic, not at home. She had been told many times that she risked severe bleeding after childbirth because she had delivered so many babies. The words echoed in her ears: "The more babies you have, the more likely that severe bleeding will happen to you. You had better go to the midwife for your delivery." She heeded the advice and set out for the two-mile journey: quite a hike for a woman in labour.

Luckily, Sophia's favourite midwife, Shannon, met her with a smile. But the smile soon disappeared.

Shannon's eyes told more than her words—something wasn't right.

"My dear sister Sophia, your baby is coming foot first! It cannot be born this way. You must quickly make arrangements to go to the hospital."

Sophia had to send word to Humphrey. Between labour pains, she asked a boy playing nearby to go and tell him that she was on her way to the hospital, and that he had to send money to pay the fees.

Humphrey arrived in five minutes with 8,000 shillings (about $4 US). Breaking with African tradition, he had rushed out of a meeting with the local chief, as soon as he heard that there might be trouble for Sophia.

He didn't clearly understand what the problem was, but it was difficult for Shannon to spell out: If the baby is born feet first, its head can get stuck in the birth canal, which means death from asphyxiation.

Sophia was whizzed off toward the hospital on the back of a Boda Boda (what the Ugandan's call a small motorbike.) It was a long, bumpy ride, but at least she was the only passenger. She had seen three or four on a Suzuki before.

The rest seemed like a dream. A small scrap of paper from Shannon introduced Sophia to the hospital staff. The staff sprang into action as soon as they read it. Before she knew it, Sophia was upstairs in the operating theatre, surrounded by sterile gowns, equipment and a strange, pungent smell.

She remembered the anaesthesia assistant telling her to take a big breath, and the next thing she heard was a beautiful 6 pound 13 ounce baby boy filling his lungs with air.

For the next eight days Sophia struggled to feed the little boy. She had consented to a tubal ligation during the surgery, so she knew that he was her last baby. She and Humphrey waited a week before naming him. This tradition is grounded in the uncertainty of life in rural Africa.

But this time, perhaps, things were not quite so uncertain. Sophia had gotten help in time, and she left the hospital with her son in her arms and Shannon the midwife following, carrying her supplies. Shannon was exhilarated. As a midwife, she looked forward to the day when she would speak to the child whose life she had helped to save.

You knit me together in my mother's womb. I will praise you for I am fearfully and wonderfully made.

—PSALM 139, NIV

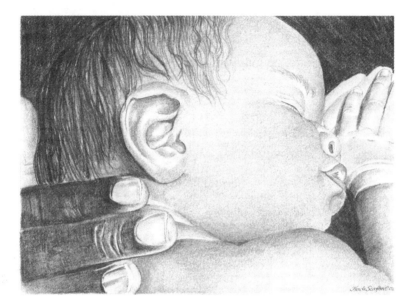

CHAPTER SEVEN

The Little Mother

Rarely do I find myself looking down at a patient. I am only five foot two, so most of my patients are at least my height or taller. Juliette wasn't. At her tallest, she stood four-foot three.

The young Ugandan woman was a dwarf, an achondroplastic dwarf, to be exact. When she was a child, her long bones did not respond to growth hormone. However, her skull and the bones of her hands and feet were more sensitive to the hormone, so they did grow. Thus, her hands appeared too big for her height, and her forehead protruded.

Despite her appearance, Juliette's parents had found a husband for her when she was 16. Because they were concerned that she might never marry, they quickly accepted an offer of marriage from Geoffrey, a 40-year-old man. They got a lower bride price for this unique, cheery girl than for her older sister, of course, but at least they got something.

She was a bright young woman. She scored among the top

pupils for students finishing primary school in her district. Unfortunately, only male students with disabilities were given special assistance, so she did not receive any special funding for secondary education, and was thus denied further study.

Despite this setback, Juliette maintained a positive outlook on life. Each day, she worked with her mother in the field. She was strong, and she could keep up with the best at hoeing.

I met her for the first time in the maternity ward of the hospital. She was expecting her firstborn child any day. She was at the hospital because her abnormal skeletal system might not be able to cope with a natural birth, especially if the baby weighed over seven pounds.

Juliette did not make eye contact with me at all. She was embarrassed and apprehensive about the attention the medical staff gave her. Everyone seemed so serious, and she could not understand the discussions.

I asked some basic questions through a nurse who acted as an interpreter. It seemed that Juliette had gotten pregnant two months after marriage. The added strain of pregnancy was making it increasingly difficult for her to supply the matoke (cooked bananas, a staple food) for her rather demanding husband. She hoped to have this baby soon and get back to her normal physique and life. Her due date was one week away.

After a few more simple questions and answers, I examined Juliette and confirmed what was already apparent to the medical staff. She had no hope of delivering naturally. A Caesarean birth was required.

My colleague whispered the news quietly to Juliette. All the other patients grew quiet, as they always did when the doctor spoke privately to a patient. It was as if their consent was also required. The patients were the first to decide if the treatment seemed reasonable. The idea of community responsibility takes on new meaning in Africa.

Juliette was told that she could go home today but must return to be prepared for surgery the day after tomorrow. An embarrassed smile crossed her face briefly. She was not used to receiving this kind of attention or information. But she quickly nodded in agreement and gathered her things.

On the long walk home, questions flooded her mind. Why wasn't she like other women? Couldn't she at least try natural childbirth? Why had God made her this way? Perhaps Geoffrey would have the answer.

Geoffrey disposed of the problem in no time. "They are always saying those things at the hospital. The doctors and nurses only want to make money. You became pregnant so easily. I don't think you need to have anything special done. My mother can help you. If there is a problem, she can send you to the hospital. Let us not waste our money on these things."

Juliette was glad to do what Geoffrey said. She made dinner, and soon they sat huddled over their simple meal of matoke, rice, and green vegetables. They were grateful for it; their parents could tell them of times that had been much worse.

Their parents had lived through the terrible regime of Idi Amin. They had been lucky to live in places that escaped the worst of the terror.

Uganda was still putting the pieces back together, while the rest of the world raced ahead into the technological age. As a result, the sophistication that consumed the rest of the globe bypassed Geoffrey and Juliette.

They were oblivious to satellites roaming the skies above their heads. As they turned down the kerosene lamp, they settled in for another warm night in their mud hut, hoping the thatch on the roof would keep the rain out.

Juliette had no alarm clock. Nature, which surrounded her, seemed sufficient. True, the roosters became confused sometimes, crowing in the middle of the night instead of at sunrise.

She only heeded their alarm when she saw the sun peeking over the distant hill.

Her day progressed like all the rest; morning chai (tea) was made, water fetched, the garden tilled, and the animals tended. In a short time, she was again preparing dinner for her husband who had spent the day in town.

As Geoffrey poked his head through the gap in the hut that they used as a doorway, he looked troubled. "I was speaking with my friend Jeremy today. He says you should go to the hospital to have your baby. He told me stories about other short women like you. Several have died in childbirth. He said I was a coward if I didn't allow you to go. All of these things are new to me. I should do what this man has counselled me."

Juliette could barely believe her ears. So she would have surgery after all! While she was somewhat surprised by her husband's abrupt change of mind, she knew how much a Ugandan husband can be influenced by other men's opinions.

"They told me to come on Tuesday so the surgery could be done on Wednesday. I will have to leave tomorrow." She asked cautiously, "Will you be ready?"

Geoffrey, as it turned out, wasn't going. He gave Juliette six thousand shillings (approximately $3 US), and wished her well.

After walking three kilometres to the nearest road, she took the commuter bus to the hospital. It was so different from her native mud hut. The electric lights dazzled her eyes, and the cold cement walls seemed uninviting and foreign. She had already parted with two thousand of her precious shillings before she even reached the maternity ward. She hoped the surgery would not cost too much more, or else she would be ashamed. Worse yet, they might not do the surgery if she couldn't pay.

I was completing my afternoon rounds on the ward when the midwife reintroduced me to Juliette. It was hard to tell if she was nervous. Despite being alone, she was bright and cheerful;

an "odd ball" in her society, yet friendly to anyone who would lend her the time of day.

Through the midwife interpreter I told her once again why the surgery was needed. She had the pelvis of a child. Even if her baby was a dwarf, it would have a normal size head. Without an ultrasound machine within a hundred kilometres, I couldn't tell her whether her baby was in fact a dwarf. Given that her husband was of normal size, it was fifty-fifty, and we would just have to wait and see.

We discussed the risks and complications of surgery, and Juliette consented with a stamp of her thumb.

Surgery was scheduled for 9 o'clock the next morning. Juliette spent a restless night in the maternity ward, disturbed by nurses taking her blood pressure and by the cries of newborn babies. The starlit African sky faded and the morning of her appointment stared the young girl in the face. Today she would bring forth life.

On a cold stretcher, Juliette was wheeled into the operating theatre, a small, thin blanket covering her naked body. She knew that no one could see her private parts, yet she felt vulnerable and exposed.

It didn't help that, as she nodded off into unconsciousness, she could hear the medical workers joking about what her husband must look like, and hoping out loud that the baby was not a dwarf. I wished I knew their language better, so that I could interject. They did not seem to realize that the patient can often hear what is said.

The next time Juliette was conscious of her surroundings, her abdomen was flat and she could hear her daughter's cries in the distance.

She could hardly wait to see her baby, but, as most Ugandan women do, she remained silent and waited for orders. The midwife, Susan, brought the baby and announced. with a smile and a gentle hug, "Your baby is just like you."

There were snickers in the background, but Juliette did not care that her daughter was a dwarf. She had succeeded in bearing a child.

Juliette remained on the ward for eight days. She spent her time learning the art of breast-feeding. Everyone encouraged her, and she succeeded. She was a treasure of all the maternity staff; a brave young mother who had dared to ensure her health and that of her newborn baby.

As she walked out the hospital door with a healthy baby girl in her arms, she whispered to herself, "I did it. I have my first-born child."

Personally, I was thankful that she and her baby were even alive.

Juliette is an example of how mothers dying from preventable causes in developing countries can be saved. She could easily have died in childbirth. But she had the courage to seek help in time, even though the hospital seemed strange and unnatural to her. No, I don't look down at this strong-willed African mother. I look up to her.

Good-night children...everywhere.

—Derek McCollough

CHAPTER EIGHT

Breech!!

Charity hoped for a quiet delivery, with just her mother and sister beside her in her small African hut. She would hear the roosters crowing and the dogs barking in the distance, just like always.

The 18 year old tried to imagine what giving birth was like, but that was difficult. People told her different things. Some women said that the discomfort was mild and the sense of fulfillment was wonderful. Others told her hair-raising tales that sent cold shudders racing down her back. Who should she believe? There was not much time to decide. She would soon be in labour.

The sun was setting, the crickets were chirping, and the fires around the little hut were shimmering with heat as she began to feel the early pains. No rest tonight; it would be a "night of labour."

Charity called for her mother, who was overjoyed by the news. This would be her first grandchild. The generations were starting to multiply, thanks be to God!

Her mother quickly shooed away the men, and then waited patiently for labour to start in earnest. She knelt beside her daughter and laid her hand on her abdomen. "These are good tightenings, my dear child," she said. You must be strong and deliver this baby with courage." She kissed the perspiring brow of her young daughter.

Midnight came and went, and the contractions intensified. But the baby was not coming out. "Mother, what is the matter? I am trying to be brave. What more can I do?" Charity cried.

"I fear your baby may be coming out buttocks first. Remember, the midwife warned about this at your last visit. She said we should go to the hospital for your delivery. I did not think that it was necessary then. The hospital will want money, and even the transportation is more money than we have."

Charity grimaced at the next contraction, then asked, "Mother, is it too late? Can we still go to the hospital?"

"Remember your sister. The doctor said that she needed a Caesarean birth. I will never forget my last sight of her, wheeled on the stretcher towards the operating theatre through the large white swinging doors.

"They told me later that she died from the needle in her back that was to give her pain relief. I never knew if I should believe their story. The one thing I know for sure is that I brought in a living daughter and carried out a dead one. I fear the hospital and all who work there."

Still, she reluctantly placed her labouring daughter on the back of a neighbour's motorbike. The ride to the hospital, three miles away, would be rough but she would brace her daughter between the driver and herself.

Three silhouettes without helmets sped through the night in the direction of the small government hospital.

The night watchman met them at the gate, and said he would tell the midwife that they were there. The doctor's shift had ended at 5 p.m. The hospital was mostly dark, and silence hung like a sheet as they hobbled to the labour area. The midwife found Charity a bed and confirmed the earlier midwife's diagnosis and her mother's fear: The baby was indeed a breech.

However, it seemed to the midwife that Charity was doing okay so far. Her cervix was two centimetres dilated, with eight more to go. Her frail mother sank into the cold steel chair just outside the room. She would not be able to deliver her grandchild herself, but perhaps this hospital visit would not be tragic, like the last one.

Two more hours passed. Water from the birth sac continued to flood everywhere. Surely Charity would deliver soon. The new day awoke. No baby, no new life, just ongoing pain. Worse, the contractions seemed to be lessening.

A new crew of midwives took charge of the labour and delivery ward. Charity was re-examined. Not much change was noted. She was only three centimetres dilated. This was not good.

The labour and delivery ward was busy. Women came and went, delivering their babies and then leaving. It was now three days since Charity had presented in early labour. She did not move much now. Her water had been broken during this entire time, which meant that she was dangerously exposed to infection, and a fever had started.

The midwife seemed relieved that Charity's labour picked up on the fourth day, and it was not long before she was nine centimetres dilated. Despite the many examinations, very little had ever been written on the chart that hung still at the end of her bed.

Another change of shift, and another examination. She was so close to delivery, why not get the process started? The midwife told her to start the pushing motion. She puffed up her face and gave the mightiest blow she could muster. "That's not hard enough," the midwife snapped. "Give it all you've got and then a little more."

After an hour and a half of the strongest effort Charity could muster, she delivered her newborn son's buttocks and legs. A look of panic appeared on the midwife's face. It reminded her of her mother's look a few days before. What was the matter? The baby was nearly out—she would give all she could to get this precious little head out.

Despite her valiant effort, his head wouldn't budge. The dangling little body struggled, as if to wiggle out. After four hours of partial delivery, no life was left in him. The midwife pulled and tugged on the body. It was like a key stuck in the lock.

For Charity, it was a nightmare she could not waken from: A lifeless body trapped between her legs.

Charity was exhausted, and her heart was broken. Was there no one who could help her? The midwife was paralyzed with fear. Why didn't the doctor come?

The midwife announced, "I have made arrangements for you to be transferred to another hospital. It is a mission hospital just ten miles away. There is a doctor there who specializes in maternity. He is called an "obstetrician." I will send for the ambulance."

The cloud of dust behind the old ambulance was the only thing Charity remembered from the glum ride. The twinkling stars seemed to taunt her. They drove through the whitewashed gate and entered the hospital compound. This time, things seemed a bit better. Lights flickered in the maternity ward. A midwife from the labour and delivery ward greeted them at the door, and assured them that the doctor would be coming soon.

By now, Charity's mind was wandering. The face of her mother was blurred and horribly distorted. She wondered where her sister was. Shouldn't she be here?

A plump "Mazungu" (meaning 'white') doctor with glasses and white coat appeared. Charity could not understand his quiet words, but he seemed gentle and caring.

The baby's legs still lay motionless between the young mother's legs.

After giving her some medication to dull the pain, he delivered the baby's head with instruments that looked like large metal spoons. But by now, she hardly noticed what was happening.

Intravenous fluids and antibiotics were pumped through the young girl's veins. But delirium was overtaking her, and she attempted to pull out the lifeline. Apart from that, she was too weak to even lift her head.

Her mother, who slept on the floor on a wool blanket, began to worry that she would slip into eternal rest. She knew by the frequent visits from the nurse that things were not looking good. She dared not ask what was happening. She could only sit and pray that the night would not steal another life from her family.

Once again, the doctor returned. Charity was strangely still. Beads of sweat lay on her brow. The intravenous fluid continued to flow from the suspended jar.

He approached the bedside and laid his hand upon Charity's chest. He waited and hoped. He reached into his pocket, and withdrew his hearing piece. Again he laid it over young Charity's heart.

He gently placed his instrument back into his pocket, and his hand moved slowly towards Charity's mother. He rested it on her head covering.

Words were not needed. His eyes told her. Her daughter's life was over.

Charity's mother had done all she could. She did not understand the medical term for the cause of her daughter's death: overwhelming sepsis.

Perhaps she did not clearly realize that the mismanaged care at the first hospital had contributed to her death. What she did know was that safe motherhood was not a priority in her country. She had two dead daughters to prove that.

She started for her village that night. There was no telephone, so she could not call to tell her husband and son-in-law the terrible news in advance. She wondered whether they would even believe her. Charity had been working in the field just a few days ago. Well, they would have to believe her, because they would have to go and collect her body.

Of one thing she was certain: Intense wailing and tears would soon shatter the African night.

> *"What I wanted most for my daughter was that she be able to soar confidently in her own sky, wherever that might be."*

—HELEN CLAES

"I will fear no evil for you
(God) are with me"

CHAPTER NINE

The Rat

Precious feared the rat.

Not the rat that would bite her toes under the blanket at night. Not even the one that nibbled at her carefully packed food in her traditional African kitchen. She had faced many such rats, armed with a saucepan or straw broom, and beaten them all.

No, the rat that terrified her was not like those. It would lie on her back, as if it would gnaw at her, if she died without children. That was the tradition in her village.

In Precious' village, three hours north of Harare, Zimbabwe's capital, a woman who died with no children would have a rat, or a corn husk, placed on her back as she was laid in the cold ground. It was the final gesture of humiliation. Such a woman had no honour, no legacy, and no respect.

When she worried about these things, Precious remembered her aunt, Beloved, whose name suited her character. For example, it was the custom of her people to greet others on the path, both friends and strangers. Of course many villagers carried out this formality with no hint of sincerity or concern. "How are you?" they would ask, without thought.

This was not true of Beloved. She was a beautiful, graceful woman who gave gentle greetings to all she met on the road. She shone with a genuine love. She clapped her hands joyfully, and her smile was warm.

Precious could still hear Beloved say gently, "You are so beautiful. You will be a wonderful mother of many children. You must work hard now, and go to school. Use your mind as well as your hands."

But Precious would never hear her voice again.

During the rainy season, a few months earlier, an overcrowded public bus to the nearest town, Chegutu, had swerved onto the edge of the road to miss an oncoming car. However, the edge had been washed out in a recent storm. Unable to navigate the soft shoulder, the bus plunged into a ditch, and rolled over several times, throwing passengers every direction. One of them was Beloved. A beautiful woman, just 24 years of age— and she was suddenly gone.

Beloved, who married at 17, had died without children. For seven long years, she had tried to conceive. She loved her husband, and longed for children. He would whisper quiet love songs into her ear as he stroked her soft hair. She hoped he would keep her, yet she was not blind to the temptation he might feel, to leave her for another woman who could bear the children he desired.

Beloved would read the Old Testament story of Sarah, and pray that God would have mercy on her also, and send her a son. But she never wasted her breath on complaints. When Precious visited, Beloved taught her how to make beautiful woven baskets.

Precious never forgot the day she sold her first basket. With a bounce in her step, Precious returned home carrying the remaining works of art on her head. Her perfect balance enabled her to carry over forty pounds on her head. Her grace and poise was like that of a ballerina.

Warm memories flooded Precious' mind as she prepared for her aunt's funeral. At 16, she was now a young woman, and would be expected to participate. She did not know how she would be able to contain her grief, and she was unsure what to expect. She could barely remember her grandfather's burial; it seemed so long ago.

Quietly, the crowd gathered around the graveyard. A few piles of rocks were the only memorial to the departed. Some heaps included a pot, crowning the rocks, in the hope of scaring off evil spirits.

Beloved's body, wrapped in sackcloth, lay there as the pit was dug. Mourning family and friends huddled close as rain drops started to fall. It would have to be a short service, because the rain was becoming steady.

The minister read from the book of Psalms, from Beloved's favourite Psalm 23, with the beautiful reassurance about the valley of the shadow of death: "I will fear no evil for you (God) are with me."

The gentle words comforted Precious as she stood and sobbed, her heart broken. By faith, she believed that God was with her and that He was caring for Beloved, even if she could no longer see her aunt alive. Life beyond death was a reality to her and to the other mourners.

Through her tears, she saw that the men were gently lowering the wrapped body into the ground.

Then there was a commotion. Out of the crowd sprang the traditional healer, Mrs. Mukwenga.

Everyone knew her. Many feared the occult powers she professed to have. Slung between her fingers was a dirty, dead rat, its blank eyeballs staring into nothingness.

She threw the vermin on Beloved's cold body and cried, "There lies the woman with no child. She is no woman at all."

The crowd stood frozen. So great were her feared powers that no one dared reach down into the grave to pull the disgusting, dead rodent away.

Tears welled up again in Precious' eyes. Her aunt was a wonderful woman, no matter what Mrs. Mukwenga might say. She thought of Beloved's works of art, the house she had built, and the many happy memories she had left behind. They were true testimonies of her aunt's womanhood.

Precious wanted to erase that dark day from her memory. She had not only lost her aunt, but had lost some hope for her own future. The degrading ritual underscored the fact that a woman had no value if she did not have children.

Would Precious' own life be remembered this way? It was a hard choice. She might lose her life by having children, as many women did. Or she might lose the meaning of her life by not having them. Which was worse?

(*Author's notes:* One option of childless women in Precious' culture is to adopt children from one's extended family. However, these childless women do not escape stigma because it would be commonly known the children are not their own.

Also, local officials in Zimbabwe and other countries try to crack down on overloaded vehicles such as the one in which Beloved was killed, but there is always a shortage of transportation, and easy money can be made from packing on a few more bodies.)

> **I don't wish women to have power over men,**
> **but over themselves.**
>
> —SIMONE DE BEAUVOIR

CHAPTER TEN

The Fire That Reveals True Love

A s I strolled down the path, the sound of Jane's voice was compelling. The golden sun was sinking in the distance, and its reflection on her beautiful face captured my attention. As the drums quietly beat, she led a small chorus of cherubs. The cherubs were her children, whom she led in songs and chants. Her voice never wavered. It was as if a microphone amplified her songs as far as the hills, yet there was no electricity near her mud home.

Her voice was as strong as her neck. The muscles of her neck were impressive and firm, the result of many years of hard labour as a child. She could bear a daily load of 25 kilograms of bananas.

Her husband leaned against the hut and whispered, "Sing, my dear children. The stars are waiting for your chorus." He sipped his tea with a warm smile. He was delighted simply to hear his family sing. He himself would chant later, with the other village men.

As the wind mounted in strength, the fire raged fiercely.

Fire had special meaning for Jane. She lived daily with the reminder of its sting.

As a young child, she had always helped her mother with dinner. Fire had such an appetite for wood! It craved the fuel as her family craved dinner. Wood was plentiful in those days, and Jane would simply rush out to get more. Scampering through the bushes, she filled her arms with firewood. She often brought back so much that she could not see over the pile she was carrying into the dark hut.

One day, just as she was about to put her load down, her foot caught the edge of the pot. She tripped, lurched forward, and landed in the open fire. Wood scattered everywhere and her clothes were ablaze. She scrambled, wailing, from the hut, in an inferno of flames.

Her mother dashed over and threw the girl to the ground, kicking the red-tinged dirt all over her face and body. She rolled her in circles until the flames were extinguished.

Jane was saved. But the fire had left its mark. Jane's hair was charred, her eyebrows were singed, and her burned face was covered in black soot.

Her mother whispered a prayer as she assisted her to her feet. "Thank you, God, for this young one's life. Let her still be fruitful and have many children."

Over the next few days, Jane's face became swollen and distorted. She was no longer a beautiful African girl. Slowly, the swelling lessened, but it was replaced by scars. Her mother mourned as she watched her daughter become more and more unsightly each day. Worse, her arms stiffened and became rigid.

A neighbour, Mrs. Lupemba, suggested, "You should take your daughter to the hospital in Soakage. Judith's daughter was burned, and they helped her. She is not perfect, but she can at least move, and help with the chores."

Jane's mother was not sure. Jane was only one of nine children. It would cost a month's salary. And what if the treatment didn't work?

Mrs. Lupemba persisted, and offered to watch the other children, saying "It is her only hope. Otherwise, she will most certainly die as an unhappy, scarred woman."

Jane and her mother walked three kilometres to the road and waited for the omnibus. They crept into the small bus and kneeled on the floor. Jane's scars pulled as she attempted to bend her joints. It was just as well that they had no luggage. The roof rack of the overcrowded bus was spilling over with woven baskets and fruit to be sold in the market.

At the hospital, they joined the long line at the outpatient department. A kind young clinical officer quickly assessed Jane and sent her off to the children's ward.

Jane gazed at row after row of sick children. She had never seen anything like this before. She wanted to escape, but as she lunged forward, she sensed the restriction in her knees. Perhaps it was best to stay.

After a while, Jane began to make friends, and the hospital did not seem so bad. The nurses were friendly, and the doctor spoke gently to her. Her five surgeries went well, and after a month of physiotherapy, she was ready to return home. Her scarred face would always be a reminder of the fire, and she would have to continue with the exercises that the physiotherapist had taught her at the hospital. But at least she could now use her arms and legs freely.

Life settled into a routine when they returned to their village, but Jane still had to learn to overcome her fear of fire. Fires were set several times a year to prepare the fields for the next of three yearly crops. Every night someone would burn off a field. Before the accident, Jane had always enjoyed the wonderful scent the fire produced.

One day, Jane went with her mother to a crop-depleted field. Together they decided from which end to ignite the fire. A large heap of maize stocks were in the northeast corner. Jane struck the match and tossed it on the pile. Within seconds, the flames were leaping. Flashbacks of fire, pain, and burns engulfed her. She could feel the flames sear her body; the crackling sounds echoed in her ear.

She screamed as a firm hand grabbed her thin arm. Her mother feared that her daughter would end up getting burned again if she fell into a daze while remembering her trauma. The staged fire was in fact dangerously close and did not seem to be moving in the desired direction. They would have to retreat.

Jane's eyes blazed with terror. Her mother grabbed her hand and gave it a gentle squeeze. "It is over, my dear. Do not let the fire be your foe; it must be your friend."

Jane knew that her mother was right. She could not escape fire. It was the very core of her culture and livelihood. She would need to tame it for her own use.

The years passed on and Jane mastered other terrors as well: The fear of curious stares and, as she grew older, the fear that she could never marry.

Perhaps she underestimated herself. She had a pleasant way about her that attracted the attention of a young man who lived in her village. He would never be ambitious. His dream was simply a family and a small farm. The money he would have to pay as a bride dowry, or kabanga balume, would be less for Jane than for her sister, but Jane ignored the social slight. She was delighted to have a man who truly loved her.

Over the years, the happy couple's children gathered around their fire at night. The scars had not damaged Jane's voice; in fact, many thought she had the best singing voice in the village.

The sun had set. As I listened, the fire burned on, and the angelic voice with its accompanying cherubs was the evening lullaby for the entire valley. My ears were filled with music. I slowly walked by, awed and amazed at the bravery of this woman who became a champion over the fire.

A slave is a slave if she refuses to think for herself.

—IBO PROVERB

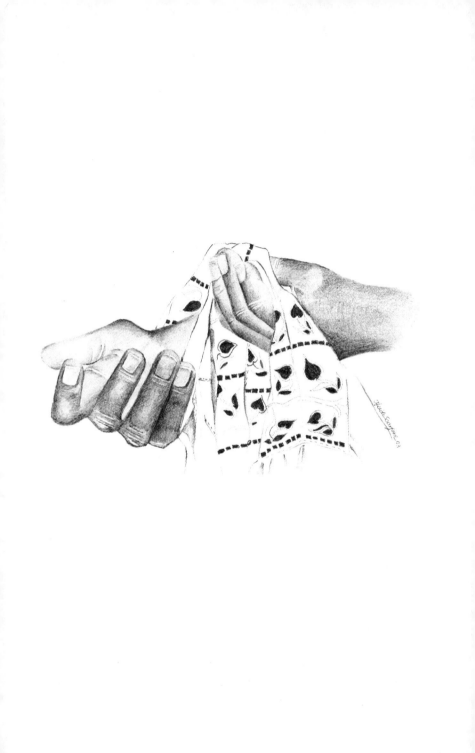

CHAPTER ELEVEN

A Skirt for a Life?

Julia was a beautiful, young Ugandan woman, straight and graceful as she walked along the dusty road, balancing a load of bananas on her head.

Her steps were light these days. She had recently met the man of her dreams. He was from a far off town called Hoima. He came from a different tribe than hers, but she felt she could live with that. And her mother would soon stop grumbling about it.

The only thing that saddened Julia was the distance between her new home and her mother's: It was a day's journey in the dry season. Still, she pressed forward to start her new life with her husband. He would earn plenty of money, Julia reasoned, and she hoped to have a big family. Perhaps she would not even have to wait too long for her first baby.

Shortly after her move to Hoima, brisk movements inside Julia's belly confirmed that she was pregnant. She would soon be wearing maternity clothes!

She contained her delight; in her culture, women do not speak openly about their pregnancy. It is simply another phase of life.

The only person she could seek advice from was her mother. She longed to stay in closer touch with her, but there was no telephone.

Still, the nine months of pregnancy raced by. Soon she would deliver.

However, in Julia's culture, a woman's life depends very much on the decisions her husband makes. Her husband—a man she thought loved her—told her not to waste his hard-earned money at a midwifery clinic. She was healthy, and should have the baby on her own.

Julia's husband was out of town the day her labour started. She sat alone in their one-room hut, in growing pain. By the time he returned home, her water had broken. She would need to deliver her child within 48 hours, or risk infection, then death, a fate all too common in her country and across much of the developing world.

The man understood nothing about women's affairs such as childbirth, so he went back to work with a promise to return that evening.

Julia laboured on alone, growing more exhausted every hour.

After sunset, Julia's husband returned home. Seeing that she had not produced a baby yet, he reluctantly promised to arrange a way for her to go to her mother's the following morning. He then went to sleep while Julia continued in labour through the night. During the night she clung to the certainty that her husband was a man of his word and would see to it that she got to her mother's village.

In the morning, her husband took her to the bus stop. But rather than travelling with her, he simply placed her on the morning bus. She dragged herself to her mother's alone.

Julia limped from the bus in agony into her mother's hut, beads of perspiration soaking her forehead. She fell into her mother's arms, sobbing, feeling each bolt of pain from the contractions.

Her mother knew that the only hope now was for her daughter to get to a maternity hospital, a half-day's journey by bus. Maybe the afternoon bus would have room for them. She needed two bus fares, but she had only a few shillings. Surely she had something to sell.

She placed her possessions in a big basket and made rounds of the village, tearfully telling her story to her neighbours. But what did she have to sell?

Finally, she brought out the precious, patterned dress she had cherished for many years. It would fetch enough for the bus fare.

She bundled up Julia and they headed out on the road, two solitary figures, one losing strength with each step as they made their way to where the bus would stop. Somehow, they arrived, only to find that the bus had moved on an hour earlier because it was full. No bus would come until the morning. They would wait by the roadside for it. Maybe someone would pass by during the night and help them.

The road was quiet as night fell and deepened. Julia's whimpers broke the silence. She was fading fast, as her pain dulled her thinking and fever set in. If she didn't receive help soon, she'd be dead.

Dawn brought fresh hope of reaching the hospital. The bus stopped by the roadside and loaded the passengers. But the signs were not good. Chills gripped Julia's body. A foul smell surrounded her. But her mother had not come all this way just to give up. She persisted in her belief that soon everything would be fine.

The hours passed, and eventually the overloaded bus arrived at the city terminal. The driver refused to make a detour to the hospital for the two women. Time was money, after all, and another load of customers was waiting.

Staggering from the bus with Julia in her arms, the mother prayed to God for mercy. She tapped on the windows of taxis, begging for a free lift. Her eyes told the story of a desperate mother's final struggle. One young man could not bear the sight any longer and offered to drive them to the hospital for free.

Julia's long, exhausting journey to motherhood was almost complete. From this point on, things began to happen as they should. The taxi pulled up to the hospital's front doors. Julia's mother ran ahead to call for help. Soon Julia was on a stretcher being wheeled inside, quietly, into the delivery suite. A kind, capable physician and nurse came to her side.

Julia then took a long breath. It was her last, as she died that moment. The unborn baby was also dead, and had been dead for a day already, after infection took hold in Julia's womb.

Four suns had set since the start of her journey, and she just could not hold out any longer. Her mother stood by, holding her lifeless hand, telling the story to the doctor. She had no dress. She had no daughter. She had no grandchild.

Julia's journey was finally over. Would anyone learn why it ended so tragically?

Somebody's mother died today. Or perhaps it was yesterday. I don't know. Did anyone notice?

—Dr. Jean Chamberlain Froese

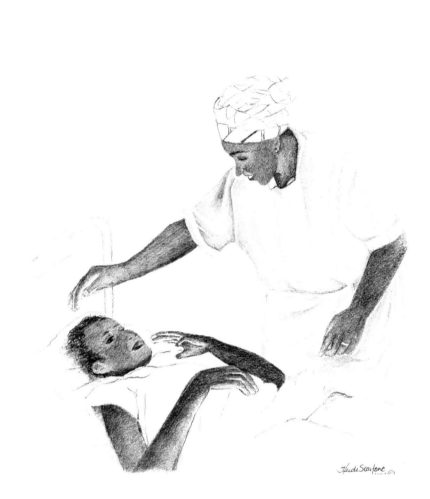

CHAPTER TWELVE

Mamitu—the Wounded Healer Strikes Back

Most women who live in developed countries do not know what a fistula is. They are lucky; they will never need to know.

A fistula is a devastating injury caused by childbirth. Women who give birth in poor countries where there is no skilled medical help may need a Caesarean section, but be unable to get one. Labour continues, the baby dies, and sometimes holes appear in the mother's urinary or digestive tract. As a result, the women cannot have normal body functions, and they become incontinent and smelly. Abandoned by husbands and family, they are social outcasts.

A fistula is a social death sentence. And it is a death sentence that is carried out frequently. Of 1,000 deliveries in developing countries, three will likely result in a vaginal fistula. One million women worldwide live with the chronic odour and social isolation of a fistula. It is estimated that in Ethiopia alone, nearly 8,000 women suffer in this way every year.

Sadly, the suffering is unnecessary. The surgical procedure that repairs the fistula was developed in the 1850s, yet it is out of reach for so many of the world's women, who lack obstetrical care.

The Addis Ababa Fistula Hospital was opened in 1975 to repair the holes—and lives—of some of these fistula victims. Often, the patients are girls as young as 13 or 14. Too young to give birth, they are left with a stillborn baby and a fistula.

The smell is so bad that the girls often survive only by working out in the fields where they do not have to be close to anyone. Many also survive as beggars. Hardly out of childhood, their life is over unless they can get medical help.

Increasingly, however, women are fighting back. Mamitu is one such woman. She delivered her first baby at the age of 15. As so often in poor countries, she had only her mother and sister to care for her, and when things went wrong with the labour, she simply suffered until she delivered a stillborn baby and subsequently developed a fistula. Fortunately, she had another sister in Addis Ababa who took her to the fistula hospital.

Mamitu's fistula was repaired, but she could not just go back to her home. Like many fistula patients, she did not have a home to return to. Commonly, the fistula patient's husband deserts her. Mamitu would have to start a new life.

Like many previous patients, she remained at the hospital to work, and became a nurse's aide. Later, she began to assist in the operating room where she was observed by the late Dr. Reg Hamlin, co-founder and director of the Addis Ababa Fistula Hospital. Noting that Mamitu had exemplary surgical abilities, Dr. Hamlin proceeded to teach her surgery, beginning with the most simple skills, and gradually moving to the more complicated ones.

Mamitu's misfortune happened 40 years ago. Since then, she has performed over 1,500 surgeries with only three failures, giving her a failure rate of less than one per cent. Dr. Catherine

Hamlin, another co-founder of the hospital, screens her cases to ensure that they are straightforward. More complicated cases are handled by formally trained gynecological surgeons.

Even so, Mamitu's success rate is virtually unheard of in fistula surgery, and all the more extraordinary when you consider that she never finished high school. The Royal College of Surgeons of England gave her a special award in recognition of the contribution that she made as a trained helper.

In many ways, Mamitu is a trailblazer among women whose needs have for long been ignored. For example, she is one of the first fistula patients to own her own home and be self-supporting. She says that she is never frustrated or tired of her fistula patients. For her, it is a "joy" to work at the hospital. It is a way of expressing her gratitude for the help that she herself has received.

In truth, her own condition was very complicated and difficult to repair, and therefore she still suffers from occasional stress incontinence. But, in her new life, it really does not matter that much. Far from being an outcast, she is a valued member of the team.

As women we must learn to become leaders in society;
Not just for our own sake, but for the sake of all people.

—C. GALLAND

An African mother sits quietly with her child. Simply due to her place of birth, this mother has a 1 in 16 chance of dying as a result of pregnancy complications.

Clean water and a warm bath are a rare opportunity
for poor Congolese children.

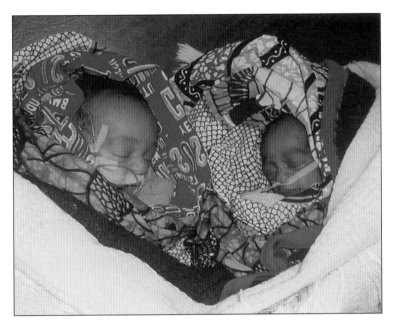

Premature Congolese twins require feeding through the nose
with a naso-gastric tube. Their chance of survival is small
because their mother is ill.

The First Lady of Uganda Hon. Janet Museveni (left) visits the Save the Mothers program at Uganda Christian University. She learns more about the program from Dr. Florence Mirembe (centre) and Dr. Jean Chamberlain Froese (right) and expresses an interest in joining the course herself.

There are not nearly enough ambulances to transport pregnant mothers to the Kiboga Hospital in Uganda.

The road to a remote Ugandan clinic called Nsala
is almost impassable.

Millions of African children are orphans from AIDS.
Mothers with AIDS are more likely to die in childbirth,
casting a dim shadow on their children's future.

Save the Mothers students participate in community outreaches. Here, STM student Eliphaz Muhindi interacts with students at a local high school during one such outreach.

Save the Mothers students learn important facts about safe motherhood, and how to strategize for lasting change in their places of influence. Here STM student Ivan Tibenkana, a mayor and school owner, absorbs information.

The Save the Mothers program is held at Uganda Christian University in Mukono, Uganda, where students can learn in small groups taught by national experts. They translate knowledge into action when they return to their communities and workplaces.

Save the Mothers graduate Hon. Sylvia Ssinabulya, a Ugandan
MP, visits Canada's capital, Ottawa, to increase awareness of the
plight of mothers in Uganda. In Uganda, she has led government
to improve maternal services, particularly by getting safe
motherhood onto Uganda's national budget for the first time.

Many young Yemeni girls are married off at the age of 12.
What will this girl's future be?

A poor Yemeni woman is in prison for an indeterminate
amount of time. Her daughter lives with her there, without
nursery facilities or schooling. How will she ever be educated?

Where Have All the Mothers Gone?

Dr. Chamberlain Froese holds a baby Yemeni girl.
Her mother will likely have another 5 children before she is
30 years of age. What will the future hold for them?

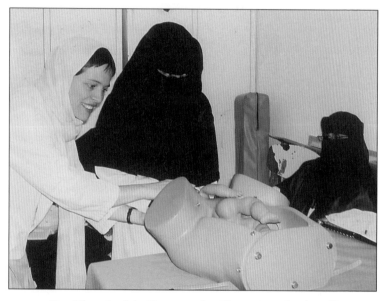

Dr. Chamberlain Froese trains Yemeni medical staff
to perform safe deliveries.

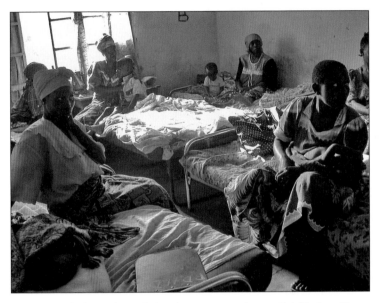

Overcrowded wards with inadequate numbers of skilled staff are the norm for most maternity units in the developing world such as shown here in Congo. In some hospitals, women actually deliver on the floor because no beds are available.

Graduates of the Save the Mothers program celebrate the completion of their studies. Empowered with information and leadership skills, these graduates are already impacting their places of work and influence.

CHAPTER THIRTEEN

Trying for Twins

The stream of blood trickled slowly out of the rear door of the dusty white vehicle, collecting slowly into a puddle in the dirt.

Otherwise, outside the hospital, the night was still. The cows had settled down, and most of the village children were sleeping soundly.

Two children, however, were not sleeping soundly. Inside the lantern-lit nursery, they were gasping for breath. They had been born just an hour before in a home nearly 20 kilometres away.

Their mother, Alisi, had been working in the field all day, despite feeling nauseated and tired. She began to worry that she might be about to give birth early.

Alisi had been told that she was expecting twins. She already knew their names too: Mbuyu was the traditional name for the first one, and Kapya for the second.

Actually, Rangani, the traditional birth attendant (TBA), did not need to tell her that there were two babies. She had felt them fighting for space, and they often prevented her from sleeping.

Her due date was sometime in December. It was only early October, so she hoped that the troublesome twins would just stay put. They should definitely be bigger before delivery.

Alisi came home quickly from the fields and sat by the open fire. She felt chilly despite the heat.

After she had rested for a while, she got up to prepare dinner. Her husband Moses would be home soon. Because Moses was well known as a story-teller, they might be hosting an impromptu gathering in the evening as well.

Moses seldom spoke to Alisi, but his eyes communicated his love for her and he never beat her. So many of her friends had told her about terrible experiences. She was grateful to have found such a gentleman.

Alisi's mind wandered so quickly. She must focus on her task: Cut the cabbage and prepare the maize. Perhaps, kitchen chores would take her mind off the problem.

Still, the ache in her abdomen did not go away. Each time she bent down, her womb became hard and tense. Suddenly, there was a flood of water. She knew that the birth must take place once the water broke. She called Rangani, the traditional birth attendant.

Rangani, arrived, carrying basic equipment such as a pot of water and a sheet. She was a pleasant woman who had received only one month of formal training. After that, she had dedicated her services to the women of the village for over 15 years. No one doubted her sincerity, and her fees were not exorbitant. She drew from her handbag of instruments sterile scissors and cord clamps, and placed them nearby. She told Alisi that she would certainly deliver that night.

The contractions became steadier; the chills more persistent. In the previous two years, Alisi had delivered two girls. Both pregnancies were without complications. She had never experienced chills like this.

The babies continued to tussle and turn. It seemed like their final battle for supremacy. Alisi wished that they would just settle and leave their poor mother alone. Surely, she needed her rest, given that she would have to care for them in just a few hours.

Mbuyu was finally born just before midnight, a sweet baby girl. Her younger sister Kapya followed within minutes, equally loveable, but so tiny.

The two little babies struggled to take their first breaths. They seemed hearty, and yet they could not breathe easily. Rangani, realized that they were too small to be cared for in the village. They needed to go to the local hospital as quickly as possible.

She shouted to her friend Fastinah to fetch a taxi. Within a few moments, a covered Toyota pickup screeched to the front door of the hut. Rangani packaged the two little babies into blanket bundles and loaded them into the front cab. Alisi had not yet delivered the afterbirth, so Rangani insisted that she lie down in the covered box in the rear.

The roads were rough, and the night formed a dark envelope around the makeshift ambulance as it swerved down the African road. Alisi lurched as the pickup jolted to a stop to avoid a herd of cattle crossing the road. The young boy tending the cattle appeared over the embankment and hurried them off the road, and the journey continued.

Then the pickup met an oncoming vehicle at a bend in the road. There was no room to pass and no shoulder on which to turn off. The challenger was a large truck, overloaded with bananas, going to market.

There was no way that the ambulance could have claimed the right of way. No siren announced its purpose; no red light flashed to clear the path. Priority depended on the size of the vehicle, not the urgency of the journey. The ambulance had no option. It reversed direction for over a quarter of a mile and slipped off into a ditch.

The trip seemed endless, but finally the lights of town flickered in the distance. It was a small town of 700 people, mostly hospital employees or suppliers. At the best of times, its telephones worked sporadically. Just then, the local telephone station had been robbed of its generator, so the lines were down. There was no cellular network.

The electric lights at the hospital were out. The generator functioned only until 2200 hours. However, the sound of the pickup alerted the midwife. She met the party from the village at the gate and took one of the bundles from Rangani. Rangani, carried the other struggling life into the maternity ward. Kerosene lanterns burned bright, and the hospital midwife, Rose, turned on the small, battery operated incubators.

Slowly, in the warmth and high-oxygen environment of the incubators, the tiny babies mustered more strength to breathe. They would both need some suctioning, and small nasogastric tubes to feed them their mother's breast milk.

The mother. Yes, the mother. The midwife inquired about her whereabouts. Rangani had been so consumed with the care of these two babes that Alisi had been left behind in the commotion and the intense darkness.

Rangani rushed back to the vehicle and reached for the rear handle. Her foot slipped in a puddle that had gathered by the door. She shone her flashlight and crimson red reflected back into her face—fresh pure blood. She hoped it wasn't too late.

She poked her head into the rear cab and shouted Alisi's name. Silence. No response. Rangani leapt into the back of the pickup and started to shake the motionless body. Her flashlight revealed open eyes with dilated pupils. Alisi had died. She had silently dribbled away her life-giving blood.

Rangani dropped her head and began to weep. She loved

this young woman. She had delivered her other two babies. And she had tried so hard to care for her friend. She had never wanted to see harm, let alone death, come to her.

Motherhood is truly a perplexing encounter: the giving of life at the risk of one's own. More commonly, the outcome is good, but Rangani was reminded of the bitter fates that sometimes overtook young women. She had done all that she could. Didn't she? The question haunted her.

The two babies were crying the morning after their birth. They did not cry for their mother. They were not yet aware of the loss they had just experienced. Each day they grew stronger, nourished by the breast milk of donating mothers, given because the hospital had run out of infant formula.

Nobody came to the hospital to claim the girls, so they were considered orphans. The hospital staff debated what they should do for them. Eventually an older woman, the girls' grandmother, appeared.

Rose was delighted to see her. She knew the children would stand a much better chance if they were taken back into their family. African relatives were usually willing to raise orphaned or motherless children who belonged to their extended family. Also, practically speaking, the husband would be searching for a new wife by now, so the twins' future with him was tenuous.

The grandmother promised to return when the twins were ready to go in three weeks, and she kept her word. She was taught the special precautions for underweight premature babies.

Rose remembers the day that the two little babies were once more bundled and placed in the back of that Toyota pickup. This time, they were in the arms of their grandmother. They were living proof of their mother's bravery and sacrifice. The maternity staff watched them from the hospital gate. Pictures were taken. The tiny twins had captured the hearts of everyone.

And their future? Sometimes it is better not to know. The

twins both succumbed to an epidemic of measles that ravaged their village some months later. Once again, the gulf between daily life in parts of Africa, and what is acceptable, is one that is vast.

I struggle to live for the beauty of a pansy,
For a little black baby's song;
I struggle for life and the pursuit of its happiness;
I struggle to fill my house with joy

—Stephanie Byrd

CHAPTER FOURTEEN

The Odour of Death

The smell Christine lived with every day was offensive. What was worse, it was coming from inside her. And there was no way of stopping it.

Christine, who so valued beauty and cleanliness, could accept the constant flow of blood, but not this horrid odour. No one had ever told her that the outcome of pregnancy would be like this.

Christine was 21, and her adult life was starting to blossom. However, shortly after her marriage, she had two miscarriages. She didn't understand what she had done wrong. Why had she lost those two babies? She feared that her husband would grow tired of all the problems and leave her.

The next time Christine became pregnant, the baby had apparently come to stay. She waited anxiously through the usual times that miscarriages occur, and eventually began to feel the little kicks that told her all was well. Surely, the bad times were over.

Well, not entirely. Christine's strength seemed to wither as the days went by. She chastised herself for not being stronger. Her pregnant friends managed to carry as much maize as ever.

Christine visited the prenatal clinic. At only 100 pounds, she was the same weight as she had been before her pregnancy some 32 weeks ago. The midwife told her to eat more meat, cabbage and millimeal. It was easy for the midwife to give this advice; she was plump and well nourished. But Christine had no access to more or better food. Her husband was served first always, and she ate what remained.

She was alone at home when she felt the unmistakable pains of labour. Her husband had gone to the city on business. She did not understand what he did there, but he must go. She refused to worry; her mother would help her.

She sent word to her mother who dutifully came to Christine's side. The day was long and the sun was hot, as she laboured, and finally dusk approached. Would she deliver soon? It seemed like an eternity of relentless, hard contractions. The pressure in her pelvis was more than she could bear.

The hours of pain dragged on through the next day, but finally, just before the sun set again, she delivered a baby boy. How perfect he looked! How can one describe the thrill of the sound of his first cry? His little face puckered with each burst of sound. The tears welled up in her eyes, and blocked her vision of his precious face.

Two days later, she awoke to find her baby's body lifeless. What had gone wrong? His breathing had been rapid yesterday evening. His little nostrils flared with each laboured breath.

The other women joined Christine in traditional laments; it was all they could do. Christine's husband had not even been back to see the baby. Perhaps he would not be back by tomorrow when they would bury him in an unmarked grave. Would he come back to her at all?

After the burial, Christine returned, as always, to the fields and struggled not to think about what had happened. Yet she could not ignore the persistent foul discharge that constantly soaked through her underclothes. Was that to be expected when one lost a baby like this?

Then she noticed something that left her in no doubt. Feces were soiling her dress. She sought out her mother. What had she done wrong, she wanted to know. Wasn't it enough that her baby died? How many sorrows could she endure?

Her mother said they would have to go to the hospital. That meant paying for a day-trip on the bus, but she could borrow the money. Perhaps the hospital would not charge them much. They had so little money. She waited three months before she made the trip to the hospital.

Christine's mother had to support her frail daughter as they walked into the female ward. The row of beds seemed endless. A pleasant nurse with a spotless white uniform and hat ushered her to her designated place. The iron bed seemed so formal, but it was a welcome place to rest. Her mind wandered.

Would the doctor examine her in front of all these people? Did they know why she was here? Did they think that, with a dead baby and a leaking vagina, she was a failure as a mother?

As the physician on call that day, I tried to relieve her fears by assuring her that I would take her to the operating theatre for examination. The operating theatre was a large, impersonal room, an auditorium, really, and it quickly began to spin before Christine's eyes. This was caused by the intravenous medication. Soon, she was back on the ward with her mother at her side.

I stood at the end of the bed and began to explain the results of her examination. There was a hole between the rectum and vagina that led to the leaking of stool. It was a problem that would not go away by itself. Surgery was needed, and Christine would need to be prepared with a treatment of antibiotics and other blood tests. I sent her to the laboratory for basic blood work-up and counselling.

At the laboratory, the counsellor informed her of the risk of a deadly virus called human immunodeficiency virus (HIV), which had infected nearly 20% of the adults in her district. She knew well what this terrible disease was. It was called the "thinning disease" locally, and it had taken the life of her best friend. The thinning disease inspired so much fear that no one in the village talked about it.

Christine had not seen her husband since the birth of their son. Before her trip to the hospital, he had sent word through a friend that he wanted to nullify their marriage. He had another wife in the neighbouring village who had already borne him three live sons. He had no use for Christine and her failed deliveries.

Disappointed, yet not really surprised, Christine buried her grief as she focused on the immediate need to be cured, and to smell like a healthy woman again.

I looked forward to seeing Christine each day on rounds, yet was constantly reminded of the unpleasant reason for her lengthy admission. Her body temperature eventually returned to normal, and her pain subsided.

I knew her surgery would be impossible if she didn't receive more blood, so I decided to donate it myself since she didn't have any other family members to donate, except her mother. One afternoon after work, I hurried to the lab. Trying to appear calm and collected, I sat on the donor bed while the technician, Sheila, scurried about making the necessary preparations.

The unit of blood was rapidly siphoned from a large vein in my forearm. Then I jumped off the bed, reached down to grab my medical bag, and... before I could warn the technician, I was out for the count, flat out on the cement floor. The next thing I remembered was a close-up of Sheila's shoes.

I lay there, helpless and embarrassed, just like the women of

Africa, as they lay helpless in a situation where they are power-less to lift themselves up. It is not that they lack the willpower or fit bodies to do so, but the circumstances cripple them.

As my mind wandered, a wheelchair, intended for me, appeared around the corner. I, the strong, young doctor, was rolled over the dirt road back to my little bungalow duplex. Resistance was useless; I needed the help.

Fortunately, the man who pushed the wheelchair was kind, not condescending. I thought of the help we offer to vulnerable women. Is it forced on them arrogantly, or is it a loving invita-tion to the place where they must go, for their own health's sake?

The black bruises on my face for the next week were a conver-sation starter with my African friends. To me, they were a reminder of the helplessness of many women in developing countries.

At any rate, Christine had received my donation of blood and was ready for the surgery. The date was scheduled. The chaplain visited and prayed. Christine hoped that she would awake from this operation.

The surgery was quickly completed, and Christine woke up in the ward, looking into the eyes of her faithful, smiling mother. Her mother had stayed throughout her hospitalization. Each night, she rested on the floor beside her daughter, with only a wool blanket between her and the cold cement.

The ordeal was not yet over. Many more days would pass as Christine continued on antibiotics. Each day she would express the hope that the surgery was successful.

The first few days were glorious; she was clean! But once again, the good news didn't last. Temperatures and chills wracked the ensuing days. Christine began to feel the swelling again. Her backside throbbed and the baths were a welcome relief.

I came to re-examine her two weeks after her surgery. I think my eyes told the story without the need for a translator. The area I had repaired had broken down.

Quite frankly, I wasn't surprised. This was consistent with her low immune state. She would never heal properly. There was a good reason for that. Her HIV test had been positive.

No wonder she hadn't felt well from the outset. Was this the reason that her newborn baby died? Her grief could only be soothed by the comfort of her mother. Only Christine and her mother were told the diagnosis. At the time, nothing could be done for HIV/AIDS.

I saw her as she left the hospital. She was a different woman from the one who arrived. There was no earthly hope. Her baby was dead, the odour persisted, the thinning disease was now with her to stay. So how could she walk out of this place with that gentle smile on her face?

There is no earthly answer. The truth is, she was convinced that she would live beyond this present life. She would live in a place where there was no foul smell, no disease, and no death. Her mother was holding her left arm, and the Lord Jesus, I believe, was embracing her right.

Speak up for those who cannot speak for themselves,
for the rights of all who are destitute.

—PROVERBS 31, NIV

CHAPTER FIFTEEN

Great Expectations

Faithful had required three Caesarean sections, because she could not deliver naturally. And here she was, pregnant again. Her mother-in-law had not been gentle in her rebuke. Surely, Faithful could manage at least *one* natural birth. Other women did it every day, after all.

Yes! Faithful would do it! She was sure that this pregnancy would be different. She worked harder than ever before. She would prove her name true. But, may this baby be small and the labour rapid, she prayed.

Still, she recalled the words of the doctor who delivered her youngest son by Caesarean birth: "You will need another Caesarean if you become pregnant again. Actually, I recommend that you complete your family with this healthy third boy."

His words had fallen on deaf ears, for a number of reasons. Her husband had not heard the conversation. Faithful herself wanted to have a girl. Besides, three children are hardly considered a legacy for an African woman. For one thing, she feared that her husband might seek another wife if she didn't bear a fourth child.

Each pregnancy had been harder than the last, and it was a few years before Faithful was pregnant again. Fortunately, her husband paid for her to see a doctor. They lived in a city, after all, and doctors were part of modern life.

Her husband did not come with her to see the doctor. He paid her obstetrical bill without question, but didn't want to hear the details. Faithful wasn't lonely, because she was surrounded by expectant mothers in the waiting room. Still, she would ask herself, does he have any notion of what happens at these visits?

On the other hand, she thought, maybe his ignorance is not such a bad thing. She could afford to treat herself to a soda from the money he gave her. That was mainly because she was careful to quote physician fees to her husband that included the cost of her treat.

If only this female doctor were less pessimistic! She could be such a likeable person if she knew how to give good news! But all her news was negative. She said Faithful would definitely need another Caesarean birth and urged her to set the date for the surgery.

Reluctantly, knowing what her mother-in-law would say, Faithful agreed to 8:00 a.m., July 5. She would arrive ready for the operation: nothing to eat or drink from midnight on the 4th. Orders were written. Faithful stumbled out of the office, wondering if she would ever return.

No, she would not return! She was in control; she would prove her womanhood. Her mother-in-law's contemptuous words echoed in her ears. Anyway, she had heard of women who had delivered naturally after a Caesarean! If they could do it, she could.

Gritting her teeth, she ran for the commuter bus to whisk her home. The minibus was crowded, and her protruding abdomen was awkward. No one paid special attention to her. She was expected to fit in the bus if there was room, but not to hold up the flow of traffic. With the same resolve with which she insisted on a natural delivery, she knocked the hips of the person next to her and edged her way onto the commuter bus.

After all, plenty of work awaited her at home. Five hungry mouths. Three belonged to small boys who would soon be home from school. Matoke (cooked bananas) had to be prepared. She would buy some banana leaves at the local market on her way home.

The week wore on. The dreaded date was approaching, but there were still no signs of labour.

She didn't breathe a word to anyone about the date she had set for the operation. In her mind, the date was irrelevant, because she would surely deliver beforehand. Why humiliate herself in front of her husband by mentioning it? He would be proud of her when she succeeded with a natural birth. She could almost taste the sweetness of her accomplishment. Just wait till her mother-in-law heard about it—talk about an end to nagging!

On July 5, the sun rose and set. Faithful did not keep the appointment. But the baby was not born naturally either. She could still feel the baby move, so surely everything was all right. That's what counted.

Two weeks passed. Her husband demanded to know why she had not seen the doctor recently. His friend's wife had been seeing the doctor every week during the final weeks of her pregnancy. Could his own wife be seen to do less?

Faithful returned to her doctor nervously. She knew that the doctor would be annoyed. And she was still determined to avoid the social failure of another Caesarean birth.

The doctor told her bluntly, once again, that she needed the procedure, and offered a second time to do the operation.

Faithful agreed to return in the morning for a Caesarean.

She did not feel that she was being deceptive. Rather, she felt that it was respectful to appear to agree with the physician, even though she had no intention of *ever* returning to this place. She could not really go through with a surgical procedure that would be interpreted by her mother-in-law as a failure. Surely, that was demanding too much.

Faithful's husband had no idea what was going on. He noticed that his wife was becoming very big, but he did not know that her expected delivery date had already come and gone.

Another thing he did not know was that Faithful had gone to see her sister's friend, who had given her traditional herbs and leaves to start the birth process.

Two days later, labour pains awoke Faithful in the night. The water broke, and labour started.

Maybe she had put in too many leaves. The contractions came, but not in a natural way. They came one on top of the other, like a flash flood, relentless and unmerciful. But she was glad anyway. Now, at last, she would prove her mother-in-law wrong.

The night was long, and the morning brought no relief: Contraction after contraction, with no progress. The midwife came and assessed the situation: Like it or not, Faithful must go to the hospital. She reminded Faithful that she had had three Caesareans, and natural birth was obviously not working.

This was the first time that Faithful's husband realized that medical staff had assumed all along that his wife would need a Caesarean! He insisted that she go to the hospital at once. His affluent friend, who owned a car, would drive them. Faithful stalled and delayed, but finally conceded.

When Faithful and her husband arrived at the labour and delivery suite, the doctor shook her head, mystified at Faithful's behaviour. But this was not the time for a lecture. Faithful must be prepared for emergency surgery.

The doctor disappeared to complete her rounds on a busy

and chaotic ward. The nurses were busy preparing the sterile surgical instruments. The husband returned home with his friend, glad that his wife would bear him another child. Soon he would know if it was a son or a daughter.

Everything was ready, except for one thing: the expectant mother! Amazingly, Faithful, who was still leery of a Caesarean section, was nowhere to be found! In the disruption created by an emergency delivery in another bed, she had vanished.

The labour suite and surrounding rooms were searched, but in vain. The doctor was amazed. Still, she could not stand around speculating. The rapid delivery room pace continued for several hours. Three more babies were delivered by the midwives, and there was still no sign of the disappearing mother.

Then, a young woman stumbled through the door, announcing the arrival of a sick patient. Two strong African men carried in the patient on a mat. Blood was dripping down her arm.

The nurse lifted the sheet from the patient's face. Could it be the vanishing mother, unconscious and haemorrhaging? Sadly, yes, it was.

Fortunately, the operating theatre was still ready. The limp woman was wheeled in, in the faint hope of saving her life. The midwife listened carefully for a fetal heartbeat. No one was surprised by the fact that she heard nothing.

The doctor arrived, and quickly scrubbed and gowned. Meticulous sterile technique was not a priority now. The uterus had ruptured. Emergency action was essential. A hysterectomy was the only way to save Faithful's life. A lifeless baby girl was delivered from the shattered womb. The oxygen supply to the unborn child had been severed.

Faithful awoke light-headed, remembering nothing from the moment she had reached the gates of the hospital road. She did not recall how she fled the labour suite, or her collapse outside, or the young woman who discovered her face down in the ditch. Nor did she recognize the two young men who carried her back.

At least Faithful was alive. But the daughter she had so wanted had died because of her determination to have a natural birth, to please her demanding mother-in-law.

For the doctor, the story showed how heavy the weight—and price—of social pressure and family expectations can be. Why cannot mothers be valued for who they are, rather than for issues like how they give birth? And if families are supposed to show love, they can't also show such harsh judgement. If they do, the prices are sometimes too dreadful for anyone to pay.

> *On the day when it will be possible for woman to love not in her weakness but in her strength, not to escape herself but to find herself, not to abase herself but to assert herself—on that day love will become for her, as for man, a source of life and not of mortal danger.*
>
> —SIMONE DE BEAUVOIR

CHAPTER SIXTEEN

Arwa—Help Got Through

Arwa, pregnant with her fifth child, expected to deliver in just another week. She would deliver her baby in her little shack in rural Yemen, among the poorest countries on earth. But at least her sister Faheema would help her.

Childbearing was very important to Arwa. Her husband had another wife who had three children. Arwa needed to stay well ahead of the other wife in childbearing.

How delightful it would be if this baby was a boy! Male babies increase the value of the family, and she already had three.

Arwa continued to work in the fields during late pregnancy. She often had to lift pails of water from the pump and carry them to the crops. The rest of her work was done with a hoe. But there was no alternative. Another baby was another mouth to feed.

She had allowed herself a couple of mornings off work earlier in this pregnancy in order to visit Jameela, the midwife at the clinic. Jameela examined her and listened to the unborn baby's heart. She also told Arwa that she needed to take a vitamin pill every day. Arwa's diet was less than adequate for one person, let alone two!

Arwa had tried to get the vitamins and, for the first month, she succeeded. Then she ran out of money. She was afraid to ask her husband for the money. He would tell her that she was strong enough without the vitamins. After all, her other babies were fine.

Arwa had definitely felt better when she was taking the vitamins. She had more strength and energy. But there was nothing she could say.

The midwife encouraged Arwa to call her when she was ready to deliver. Arwa was touched by her kindness, but she knew that she would have to pay her a small amount for her services. She didn't want to make her husband angry by spending more money. Arwa had no alternative but to hope that everything would be fine.

Friday night came, and so did the expected labour pains. Arwa retreated to a small room in the house and called for Faheema, who lived two houses away. There was no electricity, but she had a small kerosene lamp to illuminate the room.

Her husband went out to visit friends that evening and, upon returning home, he kept to himself in the other room. Delivering babies was no place for a man!

Arwa was in labour all night, and by morning, she felt very dry and thirsty. However, she had been vomiting and couldn't keep anything down. To distract herself, she sometimes thought about her helpful sister, Faheema, who kept a wet face cloth on her sweating brow. After five years of marriage, Faheema had no children, and she dreaded the day that her husband would take a second wife so that he could have children.

At last, Arwa started to feel that the baby was coming. The pressure was intense, but she was used to that. With only a few purposeful pushes, she delivered a little boy who quickly sputtered and sneezed, after a quick ride out.

Faheema dried him off with an old blanket, tied off the umbilical cord with household string, and then cut it. Arwa smiled with delight as Faheema put him up on her breast to feed. He had a few bruises on his forehead. They must have been there from his position in the birth canal. No wonder he took so long to come out!

Arwa knew that childbirth was not complete until the "afterbirth" or placenta was delivered. She knew of women who had had difficulty with its delivery and had suffered a lot of bleeding because of it. She herself had never had this kind of trouble so she waited patiently for the rather ugly thing to be delivered.

After waiting thirty minutes, Arwa started to be concerned. She could feel a trickle down her leg and knew that it must be blood. She asked Faheema to check what was happening and sure enough, Arwa was beginning to bleed excessively. The placenta was still in the womb and wasn't budging. She realized that it must be delivered soon or she could bleed to death.

Arwa's husband had gone to the nearest town to buy seed, so she told her sister to waken her own husband and see if he could arrange transport to the midwifery clinic in the next village.

Faheema ran out the door and roused her husband Ahmed from bed. He was less than enthusiastic, but because Faheema refused to let him go back to sleep, he got up and asked the neighbour to borrow their old pickup truck.

It was a long bumpy five kilometres to the medical clinic. Every bump sent Arwa flying in one direction or another. She became weaker and weaker as a steady stream of life blood poured out of her body. By the time she arrived at the clinic, she was barely conscious.

Still, Faheema was vastly relieved to see that the clinic was already open and that Jameela was on duty. They carried Arwa into the clinic and placed her on the small bed in the midwifery unit. The clinic was fortunate enough to have a doctor visit the clinic twice a week, and it happened to be the day that Arwa arrived.

He quickly placed an intravenous into her arm and started to pump the fluids back into her dehydrated, anemic body. The midwife Jameela gently removed the placenta from Arwa's womb and quickly gave her some medicine to cause the uterus to contract. Almost immediately, the bleeding stopped. The fluids were now circulating through Arwa's veins and she started to gain consciousness. She didn't know where she was and had forgotten what had happened to her.

In the meantime, Faheema's husband Ahmed was pacing around the clinic, wondering when he would be able to leave. He kept interfering with the medical staff's efforts to assist Arwa by asking silly, unrelated questions.

He couldn't understand what the fuss was all about anyway. "All of these women's problems," he thought. "They get in the way of us doing our work. There's always another one to take their place."

Finally, Arwa's husband Walid learned of his wife's emergency and started to make his way to the clinic. By the time he arrived, Arwa was conscious and able to converse with those around her. She barely remembered that she had delivered a live son, and the rest of the experience was totally removed from her memory. This was probably because her brain had been receiving so little blood while she was haemorrhaging after the delivery.

After the medicines started flowing through Arwa's veins and the bleeding had stopped, she waited another hour in the clinic. Then she was taken by her husband Walid back to their shabby little house. The baby was already on her breast, taking its first nutrients in life.

Jameela made sure that Arwa was given some vitamins. Judging by her anemic and sickly appearance, she was depleted of vitamins, and yet she now had to feed another, as well as herself.

Jameela waved them all good bye from the front door. She knew that today, she had really made a difference. If she and the doctor had not been present that morning, Arwa would have surely died. A needless death that required only simple treatment and a will to make a difference.

The greatest moral force in history is motherhood.
Childhood is directed by its love; youth is kept pure
and honourable by its sweet dominance and mature age
finds its influence regnant, shaping character even to
the end. Mother is the title of women's supreme dignity.
—THE NEW YORK TIMES, FEBRUARY, 1929

CHAPTER SEVENTEEN

Hope in the Midst of AIDS

Tsitsi, a beautiful 19-year-old student, had quit school to marry David, a primary school teacher who lived in her village.

David was 15 years older than Tsitsi. After her marriage, Tsitsi had to adapt not only to living with an older man, but also to getting along with—and working with—his other wife and her child. Polygamy is still practiced in the part of rural Zimbabwe where they lived.

There was a lot of pressure on Tsitsi to have a child quickly. After all, David's other wife had already proven her fertility.

Tsitsi was delighted when she found out that she was expecting. She couldn't wait for the day when she held in her arms the little baby that she could feel moving inside her.

David earned enough money to send her to the local hospital for pregnancy care. That meant a long walk to the road, followed by a ride to the mission hospital in an overcrowded pickup truck. But it wasn't all bad; when she got to the pregnancy clinic, she was received by some very kind nurses.

After Tsitsi was examined, and her pregnancy card was filled out, the medical staff discovered something quite significant: Her expected date of delivery, as determined by her examination, was quite different from her own estimate. A simple ultrasound confirmed that the exam was right; she was farther along in her pregnancy than she thought.

The staff asked Tsitsi to stay at the village beside the hospital reserved for expectant mothers. Many first-time mothers from remote areas stayed there, along with mothers who had pregnancy complications, because it would otherwise be impossible for them to reach the hospital in time for their deliveries. Life at the village was simple but adequate, and Tsitsi learned a lot about how to care for a baby.

Tests showed that Tsitsi had a sexually transmitted disease called trichimonas. Fortunately, medications were available to treat it. At the same time, she agreed to have an HIV (human immunodeficiency virus) test. Unfortunately, that test result was positive too. There is no lasting cure for HIV infection, which leads to Acquired Immune Deficiency Syndrome (AIDS), but Tsitsi underwent extensive counselling, and was told how to take care of herself and minimize her risk of getting other infections. She was also told how to prevent others from getting the disease.

Tsitsi knew that her baby might also be infected. Her heart was heavy, but she felt cheered every time the baby kicked her.

The big day finally arrived. She rested in the mothers' village until she knew that she had better go over to the hospital. She had never experienced so much pain as she did on the walk over, but she focused her mind on the baby. In some ways, it seemed like an eternity; in other ways, only a moment. After four more hours of labour, she lay in the hospital bed with a baby boy in her arms. This was simply wonderful; to have a child was a joy but to have a boy was an honour.

Tsitsi enjoyed her few days of hospital care after her delivery. She slept in a room with 15 other mothers, so there was always lots of chatter and laughter. Her appetite was good; she always looked forward to the lunch cart with warm potato soup.

The day before her discharge, however, she began to feel rather light-headed and weak. At first, the nurses believed that she had an infection in the womb (endometritis) and gave her antibiotics. However, before the end of the day, they knew it was more serious. Her temperature was rising, and she was lapsing into a coma. The doctor suspected malaria. She was given quinine by intravenous. The staff expected her to recover quickly.

Tsitsi did not recover quickly. Over the next few days, her temperature reached 39.5 degrees Celsius, and she remained in a coma. She also had several seizures. Meanwhile, her blood tests confirmed malaria.

The doctor began to wonder if she had another infection, in addition to malaria. HIV positive patients tend to suffer from multiple infections. He gave her intravenous antibiotics, just in case she also had meningitis. After that, they could only continue the treatment and pray. The mission hospital had no CT scanner to help with diagnosis.

Tsitsi's husband David arrived at the hospital to see his newborn son. He was delighted with his precious little boy, but quite concerned about Tsitsi. Staff quietly asked him if he would also like to take an HIV test.

David knew about the "thinning disease," as HIV is called, on account of the way it wastes its victims. People who were HIV positive had trouble getting work, and much false information was spread by the rumour mill about how the disease was transmitted. Often, people wouldn't even talk to the victims, for fear of getting it.

Nonetheless, David agreed to the test, and asked his other wife to take it too. Both tests were positive. They both received treatment for their other sexually transmitted disease, trichimonas. Unfortunately, there was no treatment for HIV.

The medical staff were beginning to lose hope for Tsitsi. But after a full week of intensive therapy, she began to turn the corner. She opened her eyes and started to talk. At first, she didn't know where she was or what had happened. Eventually she understood, and experienced all over again the joy of knowing that she was a mother.

Thirteen days after her delivery, Tsitsi went home with David. Their little boy lay wrapped in a colourful blanket in her arms. She could not have been prouder.

The hospital staff had learned something valuable. HIV positive mothers can take a long time to respond to medication, and yet they will recover if they are given time. But they wondered, what would become of Tsitsi and her family?

Three years later, they were delighted to see Tsitsi again. A healthy Tsitsi with a spirited preschooler in tow would accompany David to the hospital. David, unfortunately, was now suffering the complications of HIV/AIDS.

In a tough world where a small virus can ruin so many lives, hospital staff can easily become discouraged. This case was encouraging because, while the staff didn't save the world, they provided quality time for a family to come to terms with a deadly disease—and time for a child to be loved by a mother and father.

Mother is the heartbeat in the home; and without her, there seems to be no heart throb.

—LEROY BROWNLOW

Heidi Scarfone ©
2003

CHAPTER EIGHTEEN

Rose Fights Back

I met Rose on the plane as I was flying out of Uganda. After introducing herself and sipping on a cold glass of water offered by the airline stewardess, she told me her remarkable story in a quiet but confident tone.

Rose grew up in a northern district of Uganda, an area that had long known conflict. One regime after another came and went, but life didn't get any better.

At the age of 22, she was married to John. From the outset, she knew there could be problems. He had been involved with resistance movements, and some of the rebel factions were hostile to him. As a result, there was always tension in the air. Might they strike tonight? Tomorrow? It was hardly a prescription for a tranquil family life.

Amid the tension, Rose and John had two children. Little Grace and Joshua were a real joy to their parents and family.

Life went on in other ways. John was a gifted carpenter, and got work around town. Rose, who had attended university

151

before she married, focused on developing small business ventures. She began by marketing local eggs to higher-paying markets outside the district. Demand was steady, and local producers were delighted with the fair prices they were getting. Life was improving, for once, not only for Rose and her clan, but for the community as well.

The day that Rose had always feared finally came. Two black-clad rebels, with red scarves drawn tightly across their face, broke into Rose's home and shot John in front of Rose and the children. Rose reached down and lifted John's head, kissing him gently on the forehead.

There was nothing else that anyone could do. To call the police immediately was useless and no hospital was within an hour's drive. Her beloved husband had no hope of surviving this brutal attack.

Eventually, Rose reported the crime to the police, but she had to pay a bribe in order to start the investigation. It was just a formality. There was little chance that anyone would be caught or charged.

Rose prepared for the funeral. In Rose's society, a husband's funeral did not signify only the end of a life and a relationship. When she laid her beloved husband to rest, she would also lose the property that she and John had worked for together; the house and all of their jointly owned possessions would be taken by his family. And—this was the real heartbreak—they would take away her children too.

Thus, on the day of the funeral, Rose faced in-laws who expected to take her children and everything she owned. As a widow, she was without rights.

After a brief funeral procession and a quiet time at the graveyard, John's body was buried in a box-like wooden coffin, manufactured by a local craftsman. Rose was glad that she had a few shillings for the coffin and even for a small memorial at his graveside. She would always admire his courage and remember his warm smile.

But he was gone. He couldn't help her. And the only thing she could now do for her two children was to sob quietly, so as not to frighten them, when her sister-in-law Edith took them by the hand and led them away to their new "home." They were crying too, but Edith had a firm grip on their hands.

Rose's grief was more for her children than it was for her. Edith already had six children. The future for Rose's kids in such a large family was dismal. There wouldn't be money for school or other needs. They would never receive a quality education like Rose and John's. They would always be orphan children, the ones whose interests came last.

It's hard to be sure exactly what happens when a human being decides to fight for dignity and rights. Rose was a smart woman, and she knew she would need a good strategy to help her children. She knew better than to try and break tradition in front of her whole village and simply take the children back for herself. She would have to find another way.

She spent a few weeks recovering at her own parents' home, and then realized that it was time to take action. If she didn't reclaim her children within a short period of time, there would be no hope. Taking action meant a long and uncertain trip to help that could be found in Uganda's capital, Kampala.

It was not the bad roads and the bandits that caused her anxiety. Her greatest burden was the uncertainty, the radical newness, of what she was trying to do. She wanted to challenge the cultural abduction of her children in the courts.

They were her children, and not her in-laws'. Yet the cultural forces that permitted them to be taken by Aunt Edith were very powerful and in fact, from a local perspective, were more powerful than the law itself. She did not know of any laws that protected her or of anyone else who had gotten their children back. But she was going to try, and die trying if she had to.

With only a few shillings in her pocket and the clothes on her back, Rose arrived in Kampala and was taken in by an old university friend. Her friend suggested the names of lawyers who might help her.

However, most lawyers were not interested in charity cases like Rose. She walked from office to office, closed door after closed door. She had only one name left. She prayed as she walked up to the secretary's desk.

The well-dressed woman behind the desk gazed up at Rose and, in the most condescending voice, inquired "May I help you?" Rose explained her situation. The woman seemed less and less interested, but did offer her a wooden chair and disappeared to speak with the "boss."

She reappeared a few minutes later. Rose could see the lawyer once he was finished with current business. After about an hour, Rose was ushered in. She told her story. He listened carefully. Then, to her surprise, he agreed to represent her. It would be a great success if they could win, he said. Rose was almost shocked by his eagerness to help her, a widow with nothing to repay him.

Now to get the legal process in motion. It might be a long time before her case was heard. The judicial system had few resources, and cases of disputed property and children were last in line. Rose needed patience and determination.

As I listened to Rose calmly tell the story of how she fought back, I felt, if anything, more frustrated than she did by her lack of power and the infringement of her basic human rights. I didn't know how she had the strength to patiently wait for the judicial system to hear her out. It seemed that the traditions of her upbringing didn't take the time to listen—would the court be any different?

Far from simply waiting for justice, Rose researched business ventures. She wanted to be ready in case she received back the property that she and her husband had jointly held. She developed an excellent business idea, but it depended on getting back her children and property.

The fateful day in court came and went. It must have been a blur to Rose. She despaired, gazing at her own precious children who were no longer under her care.

It seemed so unfair. She had not lost them through negligence, abuse or incompetent parenting. Rather, in her culture, her husband was the only real guardian of children or owner of property; she had no rights as a widow.

But the court—to her amazement—did not agree with the culture. Rose got her children back. What a warm embrace was waiting for those two children! All her husband's property was returned to her. Now she could plan for her family's future.

Rose went on to buy a small business that manufactured bricks. These specially made bricks were stronger than regular bricks because they incorporated cement into their structure. They were made to outlast and outperform.

I met Rose again a few years later, and she showed me some of the well built schools that were constructed with her bricks. These bricks reflected the endurance and persistence of their manufacturer, Rose. She herself had withstood the storms and winds that attempted to topple her and her family.

The sad reality is that many women lack the courage, ability, or connections to pursue their right to family and property. Their stories often have unhappy endings. Shouldn't every mother in all societies be guaranteed these basic rights without having to fight for them?

I'm not going to lie down and let trouble walk over me.

—ELLEN GLASGOW

CHAPTER NINETEEN

Mothers at War

The flames were no longer contained in the cooking pits. The whole village was ablaze. Thatched roofs were on fire, as gunshots echoed across the valley like the sound of rapidly beating drums.

Prisca's country was at war, and the enemy was from within. Her people were killing their own. When would this insanity end? Who could bring peace?

The gentle kick inside Prisca's abdomen reminded her of the certain chaos that the new generation would inherit. She stroked her jutting abdomen in an attempt to comfort her unborn child. He nudged and wiggled, as if to communicate his reassurance.

"Life will be better soon. I know," Prisca quietly whispered, in an improvised lullaby.

Fortunately, her village had been spared the widespread looting. Only a few huts had been scorched.

War or no war, Prisca had to carry out her daily chores. She could harvest as much maize as ever when she was pregnant.

Her muscular arms bulged from lifting the load of maize onto her head.

Prisca was the sort of wife that so many African men admired and hoped to have. Even the conflict raging around her did not hinder her from fulfilling her duty as wife and mother. Soon she would add another child to their family of four.

The sun radiated intense heat on her cloth-covered head. The shovel reflected brilliant light into her squinting eyes. As the day wore on, the baskets were filling with the fruit of her labour.

No drinking water was accessible in the fields. She had to wait until the end of the day to satisfy her thirst.

The sun was now lower in the sky, and she started to walk back to her thatch-roofed home to prepare the meal for her family. She walked with her friend Jezara, and they shared tales of their childhood in their home villages.

Jezara was also expecting her first child. Prisca sensed that she was a bit worried, and tried to console her with some friendly African advice. "Your mother has taught you many things as a child: how to love, how to be disciplined, and how to share. These simple but difficult tasks will see you through. God has allowed you to become a mother. He will not leave you alone, and I will always be here to help you when you need it. Your mother is dead now, but I will take her place at this time! Cheer up. You worry far too much!"

Jezara's eyes brightened. "Thanks, mother! It's wonderful to have a new mother. Will you be there for my delivery? I want someone with me."

"Certainly," Prisca replied. "It will be my privilege. My little one will be a few months old by the time you deliver, so I will be able to leave him for a while." The two women arrived at the village just as a gunshot shook the air. It seemed that they were never allowed to forget the nearby conflict.

"I can hardly remember the taste of peace any longer,"

Prisca remarked. "Some people cannot enjoy the silence of the night. They are so blind to the many they harm."

Jezara then admitted her greatest fear. "I hope that I will not need a modern doctor to help me with my delivery. The paths are barricaded with roadblocks. No one can get through. My husband tried to go to town yesterday, but he was stopped. I told him not to attempt that again. I don't want some young terrorist who is carrying a gun for the first time to shoot a hole in his heart!"

"There you go. Worrying again! Each day has enough worry," Prisca said, as she playfully slapped the younger woman on her side. "You have wide hips. Your delivery will be rapid and easy, I am sure."

The next week passed quickly. The two women worked in the fields for six solid days, then attended church and the family gatherings on Sunday. There were no new reports of war nearby, but the villagers began to experience shortages of food from the capital. Tea, for example, was starting to vanish. It came from the other side of the country, as no tea was grown in this district.

Fortunately, bananas and maize grew easily, and Prisca was grateful to have food for her hungry and growing family.

But this pregnancy did not feel the same as her others. The baby's head did not lie low in Prisca's pelvis. Jezara's words haunted her. What if she needed professional help? How could she get through? She tried to ignore the problem.

The day of Prisca's labour arrived as expected. Mild cramping in the night was followed by a gush of water in the morning. She was a seasoned mother, and she assumed that she could manage on her own. She would not bother another woman to help her, because all the women had to work hard to feed their families.

Her husband left early in the morning. He knew that she was in labour, so he stroked her head and kissed her.

"Make me a nice one," he said, as he walked out the door, as if it were any other day.

The sun rose high in the sky as she continued to labour. The heat became unbearable and she longed for someone to moisten her head with a wet cloth.

Then there was a welcome sound. Footsteps at the door.

Jezara poked her head, saying, "*Mangwanani*, my sister. Have you almost finished your work? I hoped I would hear the voice of your baby by now."

"This baby is misbehaving. I hope that does not mean he will be a troublesome child. Please, will you get me a wet cloth for my forehead?"

Jezara found a clean towel and the nearly empty water jug in the corner.

"There you are, dear mother," she whispered as she gently placed a soaked towel on her friend's perspiring forehead. "I will go and fetch more water. I can also bring over some food for your husband and children. They will have to eat before long. I don't pretend to know a lot, but I doubt that your baby will be born before dinner time."

"You are kind sister," Prisca panted between the distressing contractions.

Jezara disappeared to get water half a kilometre away. She was hardly out past the house when the clap of guns and heavy artillery displaced the silence. The shots were close by and persisted longer than usual. Prisca hoped that her friend would return safely; with or without the precious water! Fifteen minutes passed slowly before she saw Jezara's shadow at the door.

"What is happening out there?" Prisca asked.

Out of breath and panting, Jezara loudly replied, "It sounds pretty bad. I met Joshua on the road and he said the rebels are at Kibo, only two kilometres away. We must stay in the village now, and try to escape only if we are attacked. We will be killed if we try to leave. Joshua says that we have nothing that they are looking for. But please, how are you, my mother? I am worried about you."

"Always the worrier," Prisca jokingly said. She did not want to alarm Jezara, who she saw, in some ways, as a daughter. But she knew that she should have delivered by now. Something was wrong, so said, "If you are so worried, ask Tabitha, the birth attendant, to come and see me. Maybe she has some suggestions."

Jezara darted out the door, and soon returned with Tabitha. Tabitha knew Prisca well. They had attended many village parties together. Tabitha had received no formal training in midwifery, but had many years of experience in this village. She was the only person available for maternity help for an entire 20-kilometre radius. Prisca knew Tabitha could refer difficult patients to the neighbouring mission clinic 20 kilometres away. There was usually a midwife there who could arrange for patients to be transported to a hospital.

Tabitha placed her cool hands on Prisca's abdomen. Her eyes seemed to announce the diagnosis, but she said it aloud anyway: "Your baby is sideways. Its head is over here," she said, pointing to Prisca's left side, "and its backside is on this side," she said, touching her right abdomen. "I fear that the arm may come down before the head. That is usually what happens with this type of presentation."

"What does that mean, Tabitha?" asked Jezara. "Will her baby turn and come out all right?"

She shook her head and gently replied, "I don't know. We will just have to see. Prisca, I would like to take you to the clinic, but I fear the rebels will meet us on the way. Then we will all be killed. We are going to have to wait and see."

Jezara rushed to Prisca's side, "Oh please be okay, dear mother. Please deliver this baby. I could not stand it if something were to happen to you." Tears welled up in her deep brown eyes.

"My child, be still. The Lord is by my side," Prisca smiled at her young friend's wet face. She said this, even as she knew that she would simply have to wait and see.

While the contractions continued through the night, gunshots outside seemed to echo them. One would start, the other would follow. By the morning, nothing had changed.

Now there was no mistaking Prisca's situation. Her baby's arm was visible, and the pain was escalating. Tabitha knew that there would be no further progress. Prisca needed to be transferred to the distant clinic. Otherwise, prolonged labour would lead to infection and Prisca's eventual death. Unfortunately, there was little hope now of saving the baby. With the arm would come the umbilical cord, a sure prescription for death.

The fighting intensified as the day progressed. Tabitha scoured the village for anyone who could take them to the clinic. The men remained in their huts. They didn't want to be the target of a bullet. Anyway, the only man who had a car had left for the capital a month ago and had not come back. No one even knew how to reach him.

Tabitha finally found a village councillor who owned a motorscooter. He would take Prisca to the clinic, but not until tomorrow morning. Despite Tabitha's begging, he coldly said: "I will take her tomorrow. Find someone else to take her today." Tabitha knew that the influential man would not change his mind.

The sun set again on the labouring mother. Beads of perspiration turned into rivers of sweat. Between the contractions, she shivered and shook. She began to mumble, and her words did not make sense.

"Please, dear God, may the morning come soon," young Jezara prayed, as she stroked the feeble body of her adopted mother.

As the sun peeked its head over the jagged skyline, there was an unusual, yet welcome, hush in the village. No shots were heard. Tranquility and silence blanketed the region.

Tabitha scurried to waken the driver. She reminded him of his promise and assured him of the ceasefire. She quickly prepared the deteriorating Prisca with a tightly-wrapped blanket and they all rode off on the motorbike. The driver proceeded cautiously at the many places where the roads were washed out, and watched for stray rebels in the region. Two and a half hours later, they saw the silhouette of the clinic on the horizon.

When they pulled up to the maternity unit, they were met by a fatigued midwife. She looked as if she had not slept in days. Tabitha quickly explained the problem as she helped carry Prisca into the labour suite. A stream of blood trailed behind them. Prisca was hardly able to move. Each woman placed one of her arms over her shoulders. No stretchers or wheelchairs were available at this small clinic. All paths were made of dirt and jutting rocks.

As they entered the small delivery room, Prisca collapsed into the arms of the two midwives. They deposited her on the labour table. She uttered no complaint. The midwife reached for her fetoscope.

The midwife spoke solemnly, "No fetal heart rate, as expected with over two days of obstructed labour. I am surprised that she had made it this far. I am so sorry to say that there is no doctor here. There is very little that I can do. The nearest hospital with a doctor is 50 kilometres away, and I doubt that it is even functioning with all of the fighting going on."

Prisca seemed to revive with these discouraging words. Unfortunately, that meant that her pain revived too, and she began to wail and thrash about. The two women had to stand on opposite sides of the bed to prevent her from throwing herself to the ground. These beds had no railings for protection. The midwife said that she had a little morphine for the pain.

"The rebels have stolen all of my antibiotics," she explained. "They were here two nights ago and really were very unpleasant. They want the medicines to help their soldiers when they get sick. They don't even know which ones to take but they steal them from us and think that it will assist them in their fighting. I was able to hide some morphine for occasions such as this. Dear Lord, when will this insanity stop?"

Prisca seemed slightly relieved after the injection. But she still spoke no intelligible words and Tabitha had never before seen the grimace that appeared on her face.

Blood began to pour out of Prisca, but without modern medications, there was nothing that her caregivers could do to rescue her.

She began to cry in agony, but there was no more medicine. There were no antibiotics to conquer her overwhelming infection, no blood to replenish her loss, and no doctor to perform the surgery to save her life.

As the sun was setting Prisca breathed her last, in torment and distress. She was one of the many silent casualties of the war. She would not be there to help Jezara. Would her dear young friend face a similar fate?

These brave women had the misfortune to live in a place where power and politics were more important than their country's most precious commodity. Mothers.

To bear you I had to look on death. To nurture you I had to wrestle with it. All women have to fight with death to keep their children.

—OSCAR WILDE

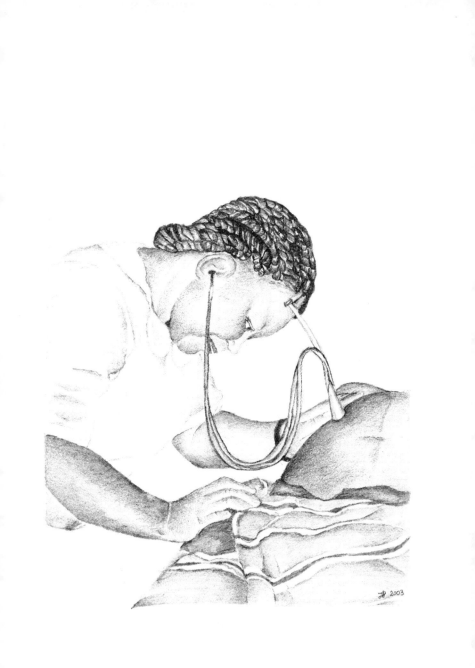

CHAPTER TWENTY

Catherine—Just a Village Girl?

Her name was Catherine. With many pairs of eyes watching her, her voice was calm and sympathetic. She answered the village women's questions before they could even utter the words, as if she could read their minds.

She paused temporarily as she caught sight of a young, black girl who reminded Catherine so much of her own childhood, barefoot, and wearing dusty, tattered clothes; a little, village girl who in the minds of most would not amount to much.

Those days didn't seem so long ago to Catherine: the smell of the open cooking fire, her daily chores, and the freedom she enjoyed to explore and play with other children.

Life seemed simple, yet she felt confined, doomed to live her entire life in the village of Nsala. After marrying at a young age, she would start the circle again by producing new little girls to take her spot by the fire.

Catherine wanted more from life, but didn't know how to break the invisible walls surrounding her. She had no money for education, and her two older brothers were in line before her if any extra funds happened to be available. Schooling was expensive; semester fees equalled a two-week salary. Uniforms and books were an additional, prohibitive cost.

Yet, she so much wanted to be like the girls she saw running home from the "Excellence Academy" each day. Their bright yellow uniforms could be seen miles away. Only in her dreams could she ever imagine attending that fine school.

One day, disaster struck her happy household. Her father was caught in rebel crossfire, and his young life suddenly ended. Catherine's mother was left with three children to care for.

Culture dictated that the children would be under the protection of Catherine's father's family. The dead man's family would now make decisions that would influence Catherine's life. Whatever they thought was best for the children was law. They might allow Catherine's mother to raise the children herself, but they did not have to.

Catherine could hardly believe the turn of events that followed her father's death. One of her uncles took a special interest in her. He thought she was a bright young girl, who would benefit from education. In fact, he was willing to pay for her education…even to send her to the Excellence Academy!

Catherine knew how lucky she was; she knew of other children who had suffered at the hands of distant relatives. She would certainly show her uncle how hard she could work.

The years of primary school sped by. Catherine diligently studied to learn English and spell with accuracy. She graduated as the top student in her class. Scholarships were available for gifted students such as Catherine, and she was awarded entrance into secondary school. Already, she had gone beyond her dreams with respect to education.

Life in secondary school was much more challenging. Peer pressure was great. Students strove for high marks but also spent much time in sports and social activities. Catherine was no athlete, but she did want to make friends so she hung around with a group of girls who seemed to have it all together. They loved to read magazines, usually stolen from a local shop. Reading materials were scarce and the purses of most students were empty.

Catherine felt torn between her loyalty to friends and the need to concentrate and focus on her studies. Two of her friends became pregnant while in the first year of secondary school. Her two friends had to drop out of school to have their babies. Their lives would never be the same, and their hopes for ongoing education would be squelched. It is difficult to imagine completing your education by the young age of 14. *At least they were able to read English,* Catherine rationalized. This was more than many of Catherine's friends back in the village could do.

This incident marked a turning point where Catherine realized she must effectively channel her energies towards education and spend less effort on friendships, which could deter her from her goal.

As secondary school came to a close, Catherine was faced with the challenge of making a decision about her career. Many of her classmates expected to work as secretaries or cashiers. They were satisfied with these careers because they expected to marry within a year. All they needed was a reliable and steady income.

Catherine was different. She longed to have a job where she could influence the health of the village women, those people whose tenderness had touched her when she was a child. Now she wanted to give something tangible back to her community. She could not envision any better way than to become a midwife and focus her work on women's health.

The entrance exams were stringent, and Catherine was concerned that she might not pass. Actually, she was a good student, and the stress enhanced her performance. She scored third out of the entire nation's entrance candidates. This was timely, because she also won a scholarship that would cover her tuition throughout the three-year training program.

Catherine worked diligently during her midwifery program. There were occasions when she wondered why she had chosen this profession—it was *not* conducive to a good night's rest. Still, after long hours of on-the-job training and study, Catherine proudly walked down the aisle. Her mother attended the graduation ceremony. It was her mother's first time in the capital city. Tears welled up in her eyes as she proudly watched her daughter receive her diploma.

Catherine's first posting was a challenge: a remote rural area in northern Uganda. Despite the less-than-ideal situation, she could not refuse, because the government both paid and recruited the midwives. Always an optimist, she considered her work in the scattered villages of this region a good opportunity to refine her skills as a midwife.

Her diligence paid off. After several years of faithful service, Catherine was awarded a position in the maternity unit of the local district hospital. Unfortunately, she saw many women who came to the hospital in a hopeless state. If only they had come in a day earlier! She gently encouraged both men and women not to fear the hospital or the health care workers.

Unfortunately, she also knew that many of her colleagues, both hospital workers and guards, extorted money from patients and their families before providing services. It was an ugly weed, difficult to uproot.

She enjoyed attending the Church of Uganda fellowship at the hospital. Her beautiful soprano voice rang out above the others, and she usually led the congregation in singing. Her gentle faith was best reflected in her loving treatment of fellow workers and troubled patients.

I watched her as she dialogued with the village women. We had come on an outreach to speak with the women and to visit the clinic midwife who operated a delivery suite, some 50 kilometres from the hospital. Catherine was now the district coordinating nurse and held responsibility for all the clinics within the entire district of 150,000 people.

Often, in African culture, those who have rank and position are highly esteemed and demand a certain respect from others. This was not so of Catherine. Despite her authority, she blended with the people, and went among the village women to help them, encourage them, and break down the many barriers that kept them from seeking safe maternity care.

A young girl in the corner shuffled on her bench. She dared not lose the gaze she had established with Catherine's eyes. As her hands clutched the sides of the wooden bench, I wondered if they would be transformed, as Catherine's hands had been. Could they also become tools of help and education for her community, so that the lives of the women whose shoulders she rubbed would be spared from unnecessary pain and death— deaths resulting from inadequate maternity services? Perhaps the next generation of midwives was being born even as we sat in the little circle at the village maternity centre.

I knew that Catherine shared my dream.

"She is my first, great love. She was a wonderful rare woman. She could be as swift as a white whip-lash, and as kind and gentle as warm rain, and as steadfast as the irreducible earth beneath us."

—D.H. LAWRENCE

CHAPTER TWENTY-ONE

Progress

By Thomas Froese

We are one, after all, you and I.
Together we suffer.
Together we exist.
And forever will recreate each other.
–Pierre Teilhard de Chardin,
20th-century French philosopher

For men, there really is no knowing what motherhood is all about. Before I met my wife, who has delivered too many hundreds of babies to count, the above quote was about as close as I could get to that mystery of bringing new life into the world. My own mother died when I was a boy, and years later I found that de Chardin's verse held something of what I imagined was motherhood, at least on a certain esoteric level.

Since then, awed and a little fearful, I've twice watched Jean labour in childbirth. And, as a journalist who has lived in the developing world for seven years, I've had some experiences that only add to those feelings, especially the fear.

Once, while Jean and I still lived in Yemen, an impoverished Arab nation where women have, incredibly, a one-in-eight chance of dying in childbirth, I talked with young Ramzy, a bright and caring enough newspaper office colleague whose wife was about to deliver. "When are you leaving to be with your wife?" I asked. "After the delivery," he said.

He was three hours away from his pregnant wife. She was a week overdue, and having complications. Concerned, Jean offered to help with an induction or C-section, if needed. Ramzy assured us that his wife Wedad had a doctor. Besides, he said, "It's better if she delivers naturally, isn't it?"

No, it's better not to risk her life and the baby's. And it's better if you're with your wife, regardless of your culture's ways. Thankfully, Yemeni medics induced Wedad, and all went fine in her delivery of a baby boy. But this, I've learned, is how women in the developing world die: at the quiet hands of ignorance.

More recently, here in Uganda where Jean and I and our two young children Elizabeth and Jonathan now live, I had a more personal scare. A friend of ours, Alice, was delivering. Jean was out of the country, ironically at an international conference on maternal mortality. Still, I felt good after ensuring Alice had arrived at a clinic safely, with the gloves, buckets and cotton-batting that Ugandan mothers are required to bring.

But later, Alice called me. "Mr. Thom," she screamed, in horrific pain, from her mobile phone into mine. "The baby's not coming out." In a surreal 911 moment where anyone can now relay his or her own death via mobile telephone, I knew Alice could be perishing in childbirth, just as 6,000 Ugandan women do every year. She survived, as did Baby Divine. And we're thankful. But in the developing world, such is everyday experience—always somewhere on the fine line that separates life and death.

In the preceding pages, I was particularly shaken by the story of Charity, with her kicking, flailing baby wedged between legs, eventually both dying, cries of Charity's mother piercing the African night. Of course, Charity's story is just one of many, and most are never told. Millions of mothers perish silently. The 1,450 women—most of them in sub-Saharan Africa and Asia—who now die every single day from totally preventable complications of childbirth are like three jumbo jets filled with pregnant women quietly crashing to earth, every day. Something like a 9/11 day in, day out, 525,000 dead mothers every year.

Whenever Jean or I have I've personally shared this information to audiences back in our home country of Canada, audiences who have advantages of modern health care, the jaws drop to the floor. In a typical city in Canada, one mother dies for every 4,000 births. In the developing world, the rate can be 150 times more. And so, westerners need to hear more: how often it's nearly impossible for women to reach a clinic; how families refuse medical care because of the cost, or cultural misconceptions; how one in four of these mothers simply bleeds to death.

Audiences need to know that those women who do survive prolonged labour are at risk to develop a fistula, a hole between the rectum and vagina that causes chronic incontinence. The leaking urine and feces leave these women with such an unbearable smell that they become social lepers. Obstetric fistulas are almost entirely preventable, yet affect about two million women in the developing world. Incredibly, the surgical procedure to repair the fistula was developed in the 1850s. Yet it's simply out of reach for many.

As a journalist, I do wonder why, in an information-saturated culture, haven't we heard more about this? Why haven't more westerners been made aware that during the two decades between 1980 and 2000, more women—about 12 million—died from childbirth than from AIDS? Why haven't more of us been outraged that more than half of these "women" are between the ages of 13 and 24, many of them girls barely out of the playground?

One reason is, unlike other global tragedies such as AIDS or child hunger, this issue hasn't been given a much-needed personal face. No film icons or entertainers have campaigned to save the world's neediest mothers. No rock stars speak out on their behalf. Even western feminists, who historically have fought so hard for other rights for women, have been silent. I wonder if this is partly because motherhood isn't the West's highest priority. Cheering "Rah, rah motherhood!" in fact, might be rather unpopular, cutting against post-modern western values of independence and freedom.

Fortunately, there are good news stories, too. And since the publication of the first edition of this book, many have come to light. Consider Hon. Sylvia Ssinabulya, a Ugandan parliamentarian who knows first-hand the dangers of childbirth in Africa. Two of her four deliveries were breech, one with the baby's umbilical cord wrapped dangerously around its neck. "But I had a doctor for one, and a midwife for the other. If not," she told me, "I could have lost my life."

Sylvia knows that the largest single cause of mothers dying in childbirth is lack of a skilled attendant. But in places where life hangs by a thread, even that is no guarantee of a successful delivery. She tells of her own sister-in-law. "She said she was hungry, and then she complained of stomach pain. Thirty minutes later, the midwife checked in on her and she was dead."

Sylvia, an influential politician, is now a champion for maternal rights. In Uganda, a mushrooming African nation with about the same current population as Canada, women have, on average, seven children—pushing the projected population to 180 million by 2050. Recently, Sylvia was able to get money allocated for maternal health in Uganda's national budget for the first time. She's also mobilized three dozen other

Members of Parliament to form the Ugandan Women Parliamentarian Association, which is focusing on finding solutions for the various needs of their country's mothers.

In the summer of 2007, Sylvia travelled to Canada to speak with Ottawa's parliamentarians and other advocates about these huge issues. Then she went to the U.K. to attend Women Deliver, the same international conference Jean was attending during that frightening delivery of our friend Alice.

How has this happened? Sylvia—and this is the good news story— has become one of the Uganda's emerging champions for maternal health because she enrolled in a new Master's degree program in Public Health Leadership sponsored by Save the Mothers *(www.savethemothers.org)*. Launched in 2005 at Uganda Christian University, near Uganda's capital of Kampala, the program incorporates a groundbreaking multi-disciplinary approach, and is open to both medical and non-medical professionals.

Students such as Sylvia represent the revolution that's possible. Think of "training the trainer." Teach indigenous leaders—politicians, educators, lawyers, journalists and social services professionals—to understand why their women are dying; then send them back into their spheres of influence to initiate broader societal change. New attitudes. New infrastructures and networks. New futures.

Jean and her team founded the Save the Mothers organization and created the Master's degree program because her experience had convinced her that an innovative strategy was needed to generate grassroots change. International debate about maternal health tends to verify problems we already know exist, rather than explore and implement new solutions.

Of the 68 people now enrolled in the Save the Mothers program, four are Ugandan Members of Parliament. Another, a local politician who teacher educates teens about the importance of avoiding pregnancy. A national newspaper journalist informs readers. Other participants are using their vocations in radio, a vital communications medium in a country with high illiteracy.

"We in the West don't have all the answers, but people in their own cultures can make it happen if they want to," notes Jean. "Even in the West, there's been change. Three generations ago, our rate of maternal death during childbirth was 10 times higher than now." Save the Mothers is planning to duplicate this approach in neighbouring developing countries, while making the Ugandan location both a regional and international training centre.

Training hundreds of developing world professionals may seem like a drop in the ocean of battling maternal mortality, this under-reported global blight that's been called "the last unreached frontier of modern medicine." But on the long journey to create safety for the world's mothers, on-the-ground torch-bearers like Sylvia, and supporters who give them resources, do give some real hope.

I'll never forget, shortly after I got to know Jean, seeing her weep for women whom she'd never met. She knew that the poorest women in the world's forgotten villages have no voice in the global agenda. In fact, Jean's parents tell me she was just a little girl when she first announced her desire to "be a doctor for poor people far away." That would have been about the time my own mother died, the summer before I started Kindergarten.

Today, others are hearing the stories and shedding their own tears for the world's dying mothers. A couple of Canadian business leaders, men who are supporting this work, equate the human rights violations of these mothers to the slavery confronted by William Wilberforce, the British Parliamentarian who, after decades of struggle, saw abolition become reality 200 years ago. "I see this (Save the Mothers) as a 'Wilberforcian' moment in time, and I want to be part of it," one of these men told me.

"One reason that many African women are dying in agony on dirt floors in mud huts during childbirth, is because they're denied the right to seek basic medical help," said the other. "The question is, do we believe that allowing African women to die because they lack basic human rights is as outrageous as having African men chained to slave ships, moved across the ocean, and sold into slavery?"

Having observed men in developing nations, I don't think most of them intend to hurt or kill their wives, or sisters, or daughters. Like my Yemeni friend Ramzy, they simply don't realize how big a difference their attitudes can make. Concurrently, too many Westerners assume little can be done because, "It's just the way things are."

So—like Charity—more mothers will die agonizingly and needlessly. But with these new voices, something is stirring. Maybe the tragic stories of the world's mothers are now growing so deep and so wide that, like rushing water, they're building into a great force. If so, the reality of Pierre de Chardin's verse— that "we are one, living together, suffering together, and forever re-creating each other"— will become more meaningful to more people. We'll realize that even mothers on the other side of the ocean are our neighbours, and care for them as our own.

CHAPTER TWENTY-TWO

A Note from Jean: How Can You Play a Part?

This book has told many stories based on the real lives of needy mothers and children: some who have lived and some who have died. Thank you for taking the time to read of these experiences that are so different from those of the average Westerner.

It's difficult not to feel a sense of anger that in the 21st century so many women are still without basic human rights, and often die from complications of something as common as pregnancy and child delivery. But sadness or anger by itself does not accomplish anything. These mothers and children need to be given a voice: your voice.

You're likely now asking what you can do. May I ask that you consider becoming an advocate for safe motherhood and joining our Save the Mothers team?

At this time of the third printing of this book, and two years after the birth of the Save the Mothers program, it now has 75 students enrolled or graduated, including four Ugandan

Members of Parliament. Also integral are health care leaders to improve access and care for mothers and babies, lawyers to advocate for women's rights, journalists to publicize the stories of needy mothers, educators to design and teach curriculum on safe motherhood, and community and faith activists to take the message to their groups.

Please visit our site at www.savethemothers.org and make yourself more familiar with this unique Canadian-Ugandan partnership. Since its birth in 2005, it has already seen tremendous progress, including new legislation designed to better protect women and children in Uganda.

Through the purchase of this book, you are already among our advocates, as all proceeds from the sale of *Where Have All the Mothers Gone?* go to Save the Mothers. And there are ways to help more. Here are some suggestions:

Donate to Save the Mothers: This is the most practical way to help. These donations pay for a variety of on-the-ground costs such as community projects and other Save the Mother student costs. Save the Mothers welcomes one time gifts, but is particularly in need of donors giving regular monthly gifts through automatic withdrawals. This helps us plan better for our future. Please see the end of this chapter for more information.

Get our newsletter. Several times a year, the newsletter is available through post or email. Contact manager@savethemothers.org and make the request.

Give away your copy of *Where Have all the Mothers Gone?* This helps educate others. Then purchase more copies. Consider the possibility of bulk copies for larger groups.

Organize a group, and ask me or a Save the Mothers representative to come and share. I am usually available, depending on proximity, in Canada from May to August. My home base is in Hamilton, Ontario, but I have also shared about Save the Mothers in most Canadian provinces.

Organize a group and share the material yourself. Save the Mothers provides speaking packages, including DVD, Powerpoint and written materials, for interested individuals who want to share the Save the Mothers story to their own groups. For more information about these packages, contact my assistant at manager@savethemothers.org.

Purchase a copy of *99 Windows: Views of a Canadian Journalist from Arabia to Africa and Other Roads Less-Travelled.* All net proceeds from this book, a collection of 99 newspaper columns written by my husband Thomas Froese, go to Save the Mothers. For more information visit www.thomasfroese.com

Offer your expertise. Save the Mothers, which is operated by a local board in Uganda, as a well an international board in Canada, is interested in developing its future by networking with professionals who might have a wide variety of skills, from web-design to business consulting.

Consider your career: Your own skills and services can help save mothers, particularly if you're in health care or education: A short-term stint in the developing world is a first great step to getting involved. You may even also consider a future career in maternal care.

To Contact Us

For any inquires please contact me at director@save themothers.org or my assistant manager@savethemothers.org. You can also leave a message for us on our toll free telephone line at 1-866-786-2350.

Thank you in advance for taking the time to care for a mother you will likely never meet. You will have touched not only her life, but that of her children, her family, and her community.

Giving courage and hope during childbirth among the world's poorest women.

Committed to help

Save the Mothers

www.savethemothers.org

Name _____

Address _____

_____

City _____ Province _____

Postal code _____

Telephone _____

Email _____

Please mail to:
Save the Mothers
c/o Interserve Canada,
10 Huntingdale Blvd., Toronto, On., M1W 2S5

Fax.: (416) 499 4472 (if credit card)
Tel.: 1 866 STM 2350
For online donations visit www.savethemothers.org

□ I'd like to order _____ copies of *99 Windows* by
Thomas Froese at $24.95 (incl. GST) each.

Monthly Donation
I/We authorize Save the Mothers to withdraw monthly
donations from my/our bank/financial institution on the
1st □   15th □   25th □   of each month
$100 □ $150 □ $250□ $500 □   Other _____

Please enclose a VOID cheque

Signature _____

One Time Donation
1. By cheque attached
(make payable to 'Save the Mothers')
2. By credit card
Visa □   Mastercard □
Card # _____
Expiry _____
Name on Card _____
Signature _____
AMOUNT $ _____

Save The Mothers is a project of Interserve Canada, a registered Canadian charity, #10679-9349-RR0001.